WOMEN WITH UNSHAKABLE FAITH

Dr. Paulette Harper

Published by Thy Word Publishing
Antioch, CA 94531

© 2023 Paulette Harper

Book Cover Design: Tyora Moody
Interior Book Design & Formatting: https://tywebbincreations.com
Editor: Emile Kline http://ekediting.com/

Self-Publishing Coach: Dr. Paulette Harper Visit https://pauletteharper.com/services/ to access information about writing your own book.

All rights reserved. No part of this book may be used or reproduced, stored in or introduced into a retrieval system, or transmitted in any form including, photocopying, electronic or mechanical, recording or by any means without the express written consent from the author.

Scripture quotations marked "NKJV" are taken from the New King James Version. Copyright © 1982 by Thomas Nelson, Inc. Used by permission. All rights reserved.

Scripture quotations marked "KJV" are taken from the Holy Bible, King James Version, Cambridge, 1769. Used by permission.

Library of Congress Cataloging-in-Publication Data

Paperback: ISBN: 978-1-7370931-8-3

Published and printed in the United States of America.

Acknowledgements v

Sponsors List............... vii

Introduction xv

Distant Faith
Shatoria Christian
1

God is Faithful, I Trust Him
Angela Harris
9

Reckon. Rest. Restore.
Petria Michelle
15

Faith to Faith
Isabelle Ramos
23

The Fight for My Life
Jackie Mungo
31

No More Secrets
Jennifer M. Jackson
39

Alive to Testify
Donna Yates
47

God Said, "I'm Not Finished With You Yet!"
Janay Thompson
55

Faith to Believe
Ebone Marie
63

Ten Days at the Feet of God
Chapri Johnson
69

The First Ring
Krystal Rosser
77

From Deliverance to Relentless
Michelle Woodson-Alexander
83

The Day My Daddy Left
Christina Aguilar
91

A Motherless Child
Choyce Simmons
97

Book Reviews *104*

Write a Book With Me *106*

Author Coaching Services *108*

Other Books By Dr. Paulette Harper *110*

ACKNOWLEDGEMENTS

I would like to express my deepest gratitude to the many people who have helped make this book possible. First and foremost, I would like to thank God for the unshakeable faith that has sustained me throughout this journey.

You are an incredible God!

To my friends and colleagues, thank you for your invaluable feedback, insights, and encouragement. Your support has been instrumental in shaping my ideas and refining my writing.

A special thanks to all the co-authors who trusted me with their stories and allowed me to coach them through this amazing journey.

Finally, I want to acknowledge the readers of this book. Your interest and support have been a driving force behind its creation. It is my sincere hope that "With Unshakeable Faith" will provide inspiration and insight to all who read it.

Thank you all for your contributions and support.

DR. PAULETTE HARPER

Visionary Author
Dr. Paulette Harper
www.pauletteharper.com

Women with Unshakable Faith Sponsors

Your support as a sponsor of Women with Unshakable Faith is deeply appreciated. Thank you for helping us make a difference in the lives of women everywhere.

Adrienne Young
Amy Davidson
Alicia Renee Reed
April Ward
Armethia Carr
Ashanti Smith
Ashley Bonnett
Aida Irizzary
Adrienne Hankins
Angel Sweet
Angela Smith
Anita Chambers
Anita Davis
Annette Lewis
Antoinette Harris
Avalon Brooks
Allan Griffin
Afira Usher
Alexandra Delee
Allison Cameron
Aretha Johnson
Anthony E. Ramos
Anthony "Sonny" & Mey Ramos
Arlene Cajulao
Arlene Zamora
Brendaria Walker
Betty Sams
Beatrice Harris
Bernard Boughton
Bobbie Carpenter
Brian Reems
Bridget Cain
Burnell Gistand
Barbara Hamilton
Brenda Wolff
Barbara Linton McNeal
Betty Williams
Brandi Kane
Brandy Baines
Carrie Martin
Carmella Carlyle
Carolyn Bell
Chivon Kemp-Stephenson
Corinne Quinn
Crystal Baulwin
Crystal Haywood-Tobin
Candi Thornton McCreary, Minister
Carla Henderson
Carlotta Bell
Carol Williams
Carolyn Dyson, Reverend
Cassandra Flippo
Cecilia Thomas
Charlotte Doss
Cheryl Widemon

Women with Unshakable Faith Sponsors

Your support as a sponsor of Women with Unshakeable Faith is deeply appreciated. Thank you for helping us make a difference in the lives of women everywhere.

Cheyenne Giles
Contessa Rancifer
Curtis Kimbrough
Cynthia Williams-Murphy
Czarina Matthews
Cela Keeton
Christy McKinney
Cristina Dillard
Crystal Matters
Cynthia Holmes
Cara Clayton
Cherika Campbell
Carolyn Blue
Charlita Rivas
Cheryl Combs
Christopher Ramos
Connie Lucero-Valenzuela
Carrie Curry
Denise Lester
Dafeney Williams
Davilyn Godinet
Dana Watson
Diane Pascua
Diana Vitantonio
Dorothy Stubbs
Danesha Gaynelle Randolph
Daniela Dana Coleman
Dannita Shellie Coleman

Debbie Woods
Deloris Wilkins
Denise Washington
Donna Steppe
Drusilla Lewis
Deborah Lantz
Debra Augustus
Debra Byas
Dorothy Daye
Donna Moses
Diep Vu
Daijha CJ Solomon
Darlene Johnson
Donnetta Lamar Brantley
Daniel Nifalar
Daphne Nifalar-Risso
Damian Broadnax
Darlene Graham
Deborah Butler
Deborah Moore
Deborah Pegues
Della Brewer
Dolores Moorehead
Dykessia Charles
Evelyn Rhodes
Elisa Marty
Elizabeth Cole Pryor
Eria Jackson

Women with Unshakable Faith Sponsors

Your support as a sponsor of Women with Unshakeable Faith is deeply appreciated. Thank you for helping us make a difference in the lives of women everywhere.

- Ethel Teamer
- Ezreonne Jackson Ministries
- Emma Lee Woodson
- Essie Jackson
- Evelyn King
- Emily Calica
- Eric & Corynna Tabernero
- Elisa Marty
- Erlinda Cobb
- Eleanor Richardson
- Frieda Molden
- Felicia Jones
- Francine Johnson
- Fantashia Sanders
- Fredrick Jackson
- Francine Turner
- Felicia Wyche
- Felisha Hagler
- Flossie Simmons
- Flora Johnson
- Flora Palmer
- Florine Davis
- Gary Blodger
- Gloria Trimble
- Gwen Sayles
- Gwendolyn Adams
- George Hammonds
- Gladys Sewell
- Glory House
- Gabriela Jimenez
- Gia Hoke
- Geneva Gonzales
- Gloria Gamulo
- Harriet Smith
- Heather McIntyre
- Helen Starnes Mitchell
- Hyter Runnels, Jr.
- Herbert Kimble
- Icelene Gilmore
- Iesha Hairston
- Janas Jackson
- Jason Clark
- Juandalynn Rhodes
- Jackie Ellington
- Jacquie Pugh
- Jada Pugh
- Jamelia Pugh
- Janice Studges
- Jennifer Foster-Jones
- Jeremiah Captain, Pastor
- Jessie Garrison
- Joan Haukom
- John Cummings
- Joi Brumfield
- Judy Julian Smith
- Judy Matthews

Women with Unshakable Faith Sponsors

Your support as a sponsor of Women with Unshakeable Faith is deeply appreciated. Thank you for helping us make a difference in the lives of women everywhere.

Janette Carter
Jeberechiah Barraza
Jereline Kendrick
Joanna Liang
Joanne Woodson
Joni Hayes
Jordana Washington
Joyce Gordon-Simmons
Judy Tonette Woodson
Janneth Nicholas
Jannette Corpus
James Jamison, Bishop
James Jordan
Janine Battle
Jephraim Brett Johnson
Jean Riley
Joseph Yates Sr.
Joseph Chelsea Yates
Jessica Harvey
Joe Ann Sheppard
Joyce Kouretas
Juakita Moragne
Jeanette Guillette
Jenean Thompson
Kiara Norman
Kamyia Johnson
Karen Ridley
Kecia Beard

Kendale Molden
Kyle Newport
Karen Lanier
Kathy Broussard
Keyanti Smith
Kimberly Rose
Kelsy Taylor
Karen Kouretas
Keeley Zachary
Karol Salisbury
Kristin McGriff
Karen Colvin
Karina Johnson
Kiana Lunasco
Kiana Zamora
Kimberly Coleman
Lakisha Hill
Lakisha Smith
Linda Cruz
Linda Walker
Lola Walker
LaShandra McConnell-Antoine
Louella Lewis
Leroy Woodson Jr
Lori Lymore Cross
Linda Gunter-Richardson
LaCherryl Veal
Lessie Williams

Women with Unshakable Faith Sponsors

Your support as a sponsor of Women with Unshakeable Faith is deeply appreciated. Thank you for helping us make a difference in the lives of women everywhere.

Libby Siino
Linda Wayne
Lisa Bacon
Lani Irizarry
LaJoy Lindsey
Lilani Medalle
Lori Alexander
Laura Larson
LaDonna Ayers
LaTonya Dominick
Lisa Stevenson
Linda Nickson
Lawan Thompson
LaTasha Comer
Lisa Slade
Lorinda Breazell
Luana Bambao
Medina Jones
Michelle Riddick
Maria Reems, Pastor
Marlene Boyd, Minister
Michelle Mosely
Michelle Roquemore
Misti Tolliver
Migdia Julme
Missy Washington
Margie Daigle
Marie Jackmon

Maria Thomas
Mark E Brown
Megan Palmer
Merry LaBat
Mona Hughes
Manaun DeVoe
Marisela Ruvalcaba
Marlen Gallo
Melissa Munganzo
Merredith Blackmon
Madelyn Lucero
Mia Wilson
Maria Cormier
Melanie Lotscutoff
Mary Hartsfield
Mikala Windham
Merian Marana Droesh
Nicole Harley
Nadine Good
Nina Murphy
Natacha Kemp
Nakia LaBat
Nanette Woodson
Nathaniel Sheppard
Nichelle Miller
Nicole Woodson-DeFauw, Dr
Nikitia Niki Hardwick
Norma Thigpen

Women with Unshakable Faith Sponsors

Your support as a sponsor of Women with Unshakable Faith is deeply appreciated. Thank you for helping us make a difference in the lives of women everywhere.

Narcissa Nelson
Nadia Monsano
Nason Tamika Fritz
Nida Dagupan
Noreen Constantino
O'Shay Richardson
Pamela Temple
Pamela Brooks
Passion Chambers
Pat Morgan
Patricia Calloway
Patricia Harris
Paul Pugh
Paula Jones
Paulette Mitchell
Pauline Beck
Pollie Evans
Phil Green, Pastor
Pamela Wright, Pastor
Pauline Hughley
Pamela Lopes
Patricia Burk
Patty Bigornia
Patricia Fulgencio
Patrick Nifalar
Pamela Marsh
Queen Thompson
Quacentia Lewis

Rhakevia Carter
Rayanna Goodman
Raymond Goodman
Rayvonne Goodman
Regina Price
Ross Garrison, Apostle
Ryann Ferguson
Ricky Brown, Bishop
Ronald Saine
Rosette Norris
Roberta Cook
Ranjeeta Prakash
Rita Alarcon
Rafael Ortiz
Robert J Woodson
Robin Wallace
Ronald Spivey
Rubina Smith
Roderick "Von" King
Rodney Pacheco
Ron & Tessie Bianco
Reuben Crummy
Rachelle Orman
Robin Jones
Shermedia Dabney
Sherry Mackey
Susan Montague
Sabrina Knuckles

Women with Unshakable Faith Sponsors

Your support as a sponsor of Women with Unshakeable Faith is deeply appreciated. Thank you for helping us make a difference in the lives of women everywhere.

Sandra Madison
Sandra Smith
Sandra Towner
Sandra Varner
Shaniece Bryant
Sharon Howard
Sharonda Clark
Shawna Glass
Shayla Brooks
Sheree Scott
Shirley Baker, Elder
Sister to Sister – Women's Cancer Resource Center
Sonya Wright
Stephanie Hubbard
Sheral Zeno, Apostle
Sparkle Green
Sharon Talbert
Shelia Tyson
Shirley Richardson
Stephany Norman
Sandie Walton
Sharon Hutton
Sonjhia Lowery
Susie Byleckie
Sokha
Sandra Randolph, Apostle
Simonette Rodriguez

Samantha Solovieff
Schwanna Otey
Sharleen Luzano
Siobhan Saulsbury
Tanelle Tuggle
Trovante Thompson, Sr
Turquoise Biscoe
Tyneisha McKelvey
Terra Dunn
Tonia Pugh
Treecy Payne
Tyesha Maryland
Tamela Jones
Thao Luong
Tina Tobin-Shaw
Tiffany Hinton
Tiffany Jones
Thomas Johnson
Tanettra Dawkins
Tina Taliaferro
Tamla Bias
Tanya Catus
Terri D. Bias
Vincent Sandra Yates
Vanessa Pouncey
Valarie Smith
Valerie Cook
Valeria Hinton

Women with Unshakable Faith Sponsors

Your support as a sponsor of Women with Unshakeable Faith is deeply appreciated. Thank you for helping us make a difference in the lives of women everywhere.

Verlee Thompson

Viana and Ka'la Jordan

Vivian Enyinnaya

Vicki Corpus

Wanda Gabriel

Winona Alford

Willie Smith III

Walter Key

Wanda Saine

Wendy Favila

Willie Robinson

Yvonne Chambers

Yvonne Scott

Yvonne Apilado

Yvonne Melton

Yauna DeVoe

Ymesa Martin

Yolanda Austin

Yvonne Cobbs, Dr

Yvonne Lattimore

Introduction

A Message from the Visionary Author

Dr. Paulette Harper
Thirteen-Times Best-Selling Author | Speaker | Pastor | Nonfiction
Self-Publishing Coach

In a world that can often feel chaotic and uncertain, faith can be a guiding light that helps us navigate life's challenges with grace and resilience. For women in particular, faith can provide a powerful source of strength, empowering us to overcome adversity and achieve our dreams.

In "*Women with Unshakeable Faith,*" we celebrate the inspiring stories of women who have demonstrated unwavering faith in the face of hardship and adversity. Through their stories, we discover the power of faith to transform lives, to heal wounds, and to inspire us to be our best selves.

These women come from all walks of life, and their stories reflect the diverse experiences and struggles that women face every day. In this book, you will meet women who have battled cancer and triumphed to see another day, advocates whose powerful messages have paved the way for others, and women who, during their recovery, were compelled to unveil undisclosed truths. Their faith has sustained them through the darkest of times and has given them the courage to pursue their dreams and make a difference in the world.

Their stories inspire us to believe that anything is possible with faith and determination.

As you read these stories, I invite you to reflect on your own journey and the role that faith has played in your life. May these stories inspire you to believe in yourself and in the power of faith to transform your own life and the lives of those around you.

Let us celebrate the unshakeable faith of these women and be inspired to follow in their footsteps.

WOMEN WITH UNSHAKABLE FAITH

I am honored to share these stories with you, and I hope that they will inspire you to live your life with unshakeable faith.

Your Visionary Author,

Dr. Paulette Harper

Distant Faith

Shatoria Christian

Sitting in a circle and listening to other women speak about their pain and hurt scared me. We were going around, and my turn was almost here. The fear was like a sharp contraction pain in my stomach. I wasn't ready to give the truth of my pain. How did I sit with other women in a circle and still feel alone? I was used to speaking my thoughts; however, at that moment, I felt stuck. I couldn't say any actual words. My thoughts fled as if I was running for my life. I asked myself the biggest question of the day: Have I ever really disliked God? I was mad at Him for many different reasons. But I couldn't say it out loud because people might see me as crazy, or maybe think I needed to be put away. Why? Because it's God. Who gets mad at Him?

Me! I was mad at Him. I was hurt and angry because of Him. I had lost faith in Him, and being at that women's encounter was breaking me down. As the other women spoke, I felt like a stack of blocks being knocked over. Each woman was going through something, and they all experienced different levels of pain and hurt. However, they told their stories. Finally, it was my turn, and I just felt sick. It took me a few seconds, then out of the blue, all I could do was yell out. I spoke the words that haunted me and felt like I would go to hell as I said them.

Being that it was a fantastic day in Tulsa, Oklahoma, at a women's encounter, I could hear God say, "Let go. Trust Me." I was afraid to take my hands off what I was standing on. I didn't want to do it. But I heard him. I knew what I needed to do, and I did it.

I said out loud, "I am mad at God. I have lost faith in Him and what He has for my family." I yelled about my hurt and felt like I had died inside. To see others agreeing helped a little, though I still felt like a wholly lost child. Others embraced me, and it was okay; however, God wasn't done yet.

I felt hurt because many desires weren't being met. In my heart, I felt alone with all the issues. My biggest passion was to get pregnant and be a mom. My husband and I had been trying, and I had had many surgeries. I was practicing standing on faith, the one thing on my list I couldn't seem to take my hands from and trust God with. People all around me were having babies, and I was planning their baby showers. When would it be my turn?

I didn't get an honest answer until that encounter, and I wasn't ready for His response. I had to be honest with myself. My faith was questioned because I had none for God at that moment. I had to see my real scars, and let me tell you, that is a very different view. After all the women finished speaking, they gave us an assignment for the next lesson. We had to write down who we were mad at. I was furious with God, but God showed me there was more to this issue. I was angry at the person who birthed me.

WOMEN WITH UNSHAKABLE FAITH

They also wanted us to write our soul tie names down. I knew why, though it didn't stop me from questioning God because my heart knew what needed to be done, but why did I have to put my business out there like that? I didn't even know the names. God has a sense of humor that sometimes isn't that funny.

When I got both assignments, I did what I was told. Suddenly, I began to remember the names of my soul ties. That hit a bit differently for me. I had a toxic womb, and God couldn't bless me with my desires until I removed some things, starting with who and what I was tied to. I had four pages, front and back, of names when I was done. Yes, it was a long list; however, it was my truth. Writing those names was an epic out-of-body experience that was needed. I couldn't believe I wrote all the names and admitted to giving myself away for years to that many people. The other assignment wasn't done, as they wanted us to write down who we needed to forgive. I knew God and my mother were on that list. They were the top two, to be honest. I wrote their names along with my father for being absent, my grandfather for leaving me on Earth, and many others. I wrote 'til God said, "Stop writing." I looked down, and honestly, I couldn't remember writing the names staring me right in the face.

They brought a big wooden cross into the room. It looked like an original cross made from a fresh, beautiful piece of splintered dark wood. All I could think about was Jesus on the cross when I saw it being carried. They instructed us on what we needed to do with the papers. They spoke so many words, but I blanked out, and all I heard was, "Nail it to the cross." It was like God speaking to me. I watched people go up and nail their papers to the cross. As before, I was scared when my turn came. Sharp contraction pains seared my stomach again, but I walked up there, ready to go. They gave me a nail as big as my thumb and as long as my pointer finger.

I started to nail, and as I nailed, I cried. I screamed about who I was mad at and why. I yelled about my hurt and pain. "I'm tired of feeling like I'm carrying everything on my shoulders for everyone. I'm tired. I feel like God left me alone!" I don't remember anything besides being picked up off the floor after that. A good friend said I left it all at the cross. When I turned to look at my spot, I noticed I nailed the paper in the middle of the cross, and the nail was bent in the middle. So I really had left everything nailed at the cross.

I finally felt like God heard me, and I heard Him. He was never mad at me, and I was on the road to recovering my faith. I finally went to my mother months later and talked. Forgiveness was the key to recovery. With that forgiveness and taking my hands off my desires, they started to flow. My relationship with my mom flourished. I needed to forgive my mother and have faith in our relationship. I also learned she needed that forgiveness. We spoke in April. I was pregnant by July but had a miscarriage. I didn't even get mad at God because my faith had grown. We ended up doing in vitro fertilization with my mother's support, and I found out I was pregnant in November 2013. My mother fell ill two weeks later, passing away in January 2014.

This was important for me because I had my mother for nine months. It was time to give back that which was taken because of unforgiveness. But I didn't lose my mother through death, I gained an angel, who I know got me. I have my daughter because I decided through the pain to forgive God and others. Because of the forgiveness, I received my desires, I just had to walk in faith and trust God. You can't have faith and not trust God. That's drinking oil and water, and it's not good for your body.

About the Author

Shatoria L. Christian is a woman of faith. With writing, she uses her voice for issues that have played significant roles in her life. She has published her first book, *Authentic Transparency: Forgiveness to Freedom*, and she has co-authored an anthology, *Women with Unshakable Faith*, releasing in April 2023. In addition to writing, she currently serves as the voice and creator of the I Am Shatoria brand and podcast.

Shatoria is a wife to Jerone, and a mom to two, Jamorian and Janae. She has currently served over twenty years with her son in the United States Air Force. She graduated from Columbia Southern University in 2019 with a Bachelor of Science in Business Administration and is currently working on a Master of Business at American Military University with graduation expected in May 2023.

Connect with Shatoria

- Website: iamshatoria.com

- Email:info@iamshatoria.com

- IG: iam_shatoria

- Podcast visual: Youtube.com/@iamshatoria

- Podcast audio: iamshatoria.podbean.com

God is Faithful, I Trust Him

Angela Harris

A little over a year ago, I was found unconscious in my home. A harrowing fight for my life put me in the ICU for weeks. As I slowly awakened, I found myself lying in a hospital bed and affixed to tubes, awestruck at my inability to walk and my difficulty communicating. Though it was unusual for me to not be at my clinic working, I was told it took almost three days for someone to find me in my home and call for help. Paramedics drove me to the hospital, not knowing if I would survive.

My family members were contacted, and they flew in for the emergency, unaware of all the circumstances. Upon their arrival, my condition was uncertain. I remained unconscious for weeks. After I woke up, it was another two weeks before I was released from the hospital. My clinic was closed until further notice. I came home on a stretcher and was placed in a wheelchair, labeled broken, fractured, and disabled from a chronic illness. My whole body was compromised, rendering me completely reliant on others. But I had to start gaining my independence back by managing one moment at a time. I had to keep telling myself "God is faithful, I trust Him."

I was determined to recover. The process began with a multitude of daily home visits. Health and wellness staff encouraged mobility, beginning with standing, and slow, clear speech. They provided diversity in different methods of healing that I was not accustomed to personally. Following protocols from physicians and specialized treatments, eventually, I progressed from a wheelchair to using a walker throughout my house. My delightful daughter helped until I advanced to using a cane consistently on my own. Continuing my repetitive health and wellness routine eventually enabled me to reopen my clinic, though I only performed light-duty tasks. Work gave me purpose and assisted in my rapid recovery.

Prior to this medical challenge, I had been healthy and living a holistic lifestyle, so dealing with traditional medicine was completely different for me. Before this immobilization, I had experienced infrequent back pain, a few injuries, and some discomfort at times. I had seen my doctor, but I received no clear diagnosis. So, I managed my health and wellness holistically like I always had, believing in what I had practiced for over thirty years. However, COVID changed everything. The availability of consistent health and wellness appointments became a challenge. Sometimes they were canceled due to restrictions. For these reasons, if discomfort occurred, I would take ibuprofen and reduce my clinic schedule. Even with the inconsistent appointments, I believe my staunch attention to my health provided my body the reserves it needed to sustain me those three days until I was found.

Throughout my healing process, I was determined to reassess all aspects of my life to adjust spiritually, emotionally, mentally, and financially. This included family, business, relationships, and the community I served. Everything had to adapt or be modified based on my limitations. What should I do? How do I manage all of this? "But the Comforter, which is the Holy Ghost, whom the Father will send in my name, he shall teach you all things, and bring all things to your remembrance, whatsoever I have said unto you" (John 14:26 KJV).

All things considered, although I was physically fragile at this time in my life, my spiritual foundation was solid in God. My belief system kept me trusting in God and reliant upon my relationship with Him.

I am grateful for the foundation of God throughout my life. His love provided the unshakeable devotion to discovering what God had already given me. I did not question my trust in God. All I had to do was focus on my part.

Due to my chronic illness, all my relationships changed. Healthy conversations had to occur based on my medical challenge and capacity, as well as my limitations during recovery. I trusted God and the Holy Spirit to know what to do and how to manage. My spiritual growth during this period was immense, intense, and painful, but it revealed the Holy Spirit's power to me. God is faithful and I trust Him.

Bible study helped me manage the ups and downs of my condition. Rather than accept others' negative opinions about my potential to recover, I continued, believing in God's promises, and only listened to what He spoke to me. A helpful scripture, which I used daily to align my emotional stamina and mental fortitude, was "But the fruit of the Spirit is love, joy, peace, longsuffering, gentleness, goodness, faith, meekness, temperance: against such there is no law" (Galatians 5:22-23 KJV).

In addition to God and the Bible, one of the tools I used during my recovery was my first book as a published author, *Wellness of Life: Whole Body Wellness with Ease*. God's divine inspiration in writing my first book prior to my illness prepared me to handle the medical challenge. And the book helped me stay consistent and productive when progressing in my strenuous rehabilitation.

My faith and hard work paid off. Seven months ago, I received results confirming the chronic illness was gone. Hallelujah!

I share my story to give those of you experiencing some type of chronic illness the belief that you can be healed from it. Your life doesn't have to stop just because you're facing a diagnosis others might not have survived.

Those of you who are reading this, I hope you know that God's love and faithfulness, along with courage, determination, and a new perspective on life can change your outcome. I encourage you to read some quotes from my first book, or find some affirmations, and speak those over your life, or maybe you have some favorite scriptures to pray on.

My illness came to destroy me, but my unshakeable faith sustained me so I could tell others that they can overcome anything in life.

God is faithful, Trust Him.

About the Author

Angela Harris was born in Western Europe, raised in Anchorage, Alaska, and relocated to Sacramento, California, twenty years ago. She is the founder of Wellness of Life Restoration Clinic, specializing in the digestive system.

Harris has been dedicated to serving the health and wellness industry for thirty years, an established entrepreneur for twenty-five years, and a public speaker for business, health, and wellness. Her individualized approach turns her clients' experiences of healthcare into self-care. Her legacy of love is shared with her daughter, son, and two grandchildren.

In 2020, she authored *Wellness of Life: Whole Body Wellness with Ease* and co-authored an anthology, *Women with Unshakable Faith*, in 2023.

Connect with Angela

- Wellness of Life Restoration Clinic, 5120 J. Street, #G Sacramento, CA 95819

- Website: wellnessoflifeproducts.com

- Email: wellnessoflife@gmail.com

- Instagram: livewellnessoflife

Reckon. Rest. Restore.

Petria Michelle

"So I will restore to you the years that the swarming locust has eaten, The crawling locust, The consuming locust, And the chewing locust, My great army which I sent among you." (Joel 2:25 NKJV)

What is the most difficult thing you have had to reckon with in your life so far? For me, it was the reality of having to rebuild my life at forty-five years old. In 2013, I had to handle a lot all at once. It was as if a levee had broken in the delta, and I was trying not to drown from it all. I was a broke, unemployed homemaker headed for foreclosure.

There was no secret stash of money, and my child and spousal support were being delayed for four months. I pawned my jewelry, including what I had inherited from my mother. My thick, waist-length hair began breaking off and falling out. However, the worst part was sharing 50/50 custody of my three young sons and transitioning from homemaker to a working single mom. It broke my heart to not see or hug my sons daily as if I was only their mother fifty percent of the time. Oh, how I cried myself to sleep every night my sons were away from me. It was too much to bear, and I had to give it to God. Either I would trust God, or I would lose my mind.

I knew God would restore everything I had lost. He would take care of me and the boys, but I didn't know what that might look like. Although I knew this to be true, when I gazed into the dark tunnel I had stepped into, hopelessness crept into my mind.

Could you handle having to reckon with rebuilding your life right now, or are you in need of rest?

"But those who wait on the LORD Shall renew their strength; They shall mount up with wings like eagles, They shall run and not be weary, They shall walk and not faint" (Isaiah 40:31 NKJV). Thankfully, I didn't have long to wait. God is faithful, and He encamped me with his angels. These angels helped me keep my faith and stay close to God during that challenging time. The first two manifested as a spiritual life transformation coach and a Christian mentor. My mentor urged me to write personal mission statements that aligned with God's Word in every area of my life: spiritual, physical, emotional, financial, social, and mental. My life coach taught me about manifestation, recognizing my hidden limiting beliefs, and how to apply faith and spiritual laws to overcome them. She taught me the power of visualization, affirmations, meditation, and combining goal setting with scriptures and my personal mission statements.

God used those two angels to remind me of who I am in Christ. They helped me stay strong and walk in faith instead of fear by applying "For God has not given us a spirit of fear, but of power and of love and of a sound mind" (2 Timothy 1:7 NKJV) to my life. More angels showed up as my siblings and two childhood friends. Although I never asked for anything, they blessed me with storage space, a cell phone, a computer, and groceries. One attended court with me, cooked for my sons and me, and occasionally filled my gas-guzzling SUV so I could take my sons to school. Another helped with attorney fees and encouraged me to enroll in graduate school.

I remembered that I am the daughter of the Most High God. The God who is the same yesterday, today, and forevermore. The God who supplies all my needs and with whom all things are possible. God had not forgotten about me, and He captured every one of my tears. I began to intensely focus on scripture and meditate on "For I know the thoughts that I think toward you, says the Lord, thoughts of peace and not of evil, to give you a future and a hope" (Jeremiah 29:11 NKJV) and "being confident of this very thing, that He who has begun a good work in you will complete it until the day of Jesus Christ" (Philippians 1:6 NKJV). Hallelujah! I began focusing on my future and the hope I have in Christ Jesus.

Who would you turn to if you needed to rebuild your life right now? Would they point you toward God?

My personal growth work with angels was complete, and God proved his Word with signs, wonders, miracles, and manifestations. Twice, I received unexpected checks in the mail for something I had allegedly overpaid months prior. On occasion, I would open a drawer and money would be there. Different drawers at different times. One day, I was looking through my mother's jewelry box, as I often did in the years immediately following her passing, and I found money that hadn't been there before. I received notice of an inheritance and property I didn't know about. One year after the separation, I enrolled in an accelerated master's degree program, and I was hired for a full-time teaching position. The school district gave me full credit for my previous years of teaching. My boss helped me advance my career to educational leadership by recommending me to an elite educational leadership program, and I was accepted. The program covered my tuition and preliminary administrative credential fee. Since then, I have worked as a vice principal, assistant principal, and elementary school principal. To God be the GLORY!

The blessings did not stop with my career. God allowed me to purchase a single-family home. Although it's significantly smaller than the 4,000-square-foot, six-bedroom, five-bathroom house that I called home for twelve years, the four-bedroom, three-bathroom home I bought was on a great lot in a beautiful neighborhood. While working with the life coach after my separation, I had set a financial goal of homeownership. Specifically, I wrote that I would be a homeowner by a specific date and year. Indeed, my home closed one day before that goal date. Glory! Hallelujah! Seven months after purchasing my home, the other house was foreclosed upon and sold at auction. That's right, God delayed that foreclosure for four years. Saying goodbye to that house was emotional for my sons and me, but moving out of it the same year my divorce was finalized closed that chapter and introduced another. January 2023 made ten years since I filed for legal separation from my first husband. It has been a decade full of more joy than pain and more blessings than lessons. Last year, I married the love of my life. We are planning to travel the world and see the destinations on our bucket lists. Thank you, Lord, for renewal and restoration!

Faith in God is a choice. It is a decision to trust that He has a great plan for our lives. It is having a relationship with Jesus, and meeting and communing with God in our secret places. We become strong and unshakeable when we know who we are in Christ. For me, becoming that woman meant divorcing my husband of seventeen years, doing a deep inward dive, and looking at my hidden limiting beliefs. It also meant that I humbled myself by listening to and learning from a life coach and a mentor.

Invest the time, money, and energy it takes to learn about God and yourself by reading the Bible and creating personal mission statements and goals that align with God's Word. Always remember to check in with yourself and ask yourself soul-searching questions. Questions that bring you closer to God's Holy Spirit, which dwells in us and brings us closer to our divine purpose. Take a moment right now and ask yourself: What is restoration? How does it look and feel? How can I find rest and restoration in God for the challenges I am currently facing? How does renewing my mind lead to the restoration of my spirit, soul, and body? What are three scriptures I will read aloud for daily affirmation? How do I allow God's love, grace, and mercy to be exemplified through me? If God exalts me, will I give Him honor and glory?

About the Author

First time author Petria Michelle has contributed to an anthology *Women with Unshakable Faith* releasing in April 2023. Petria is a wife, mother, bonus Nana, licensed Christian minister, licensed Christian counselor, and 4th generation K-12 educator. Petria is also a third generation HBCU alumna with a Bachelor of Science in Organizational Management and minor in Healthcare Administration and Planning from Fisk University.

Petria is a proud Bay Area native with a special place in her heart for Nashville, Tennessee. Petria lives in Northern California with her husband and two of their five sons. She has always had a passion for writing and storytelling. Petria began publicly reciting poetry at age 8 and writing short stories at age 11. Petria enjoys traveling, writing, cooking, attending concerts, going to the opera, and cheering loudly during her sons' games. Poetry and personal development are her favorite genres to read.

Connect with Petria

- Email her at authorpetriamichelle@gmail.com

- Follow "Petria Michelle" on Facebook

Faith to Faith

Isabelle Ramos

I never imagined nor was I prepared for what was to happen on October 10, 2010. My world was turned upside down. My husband, Anthony, came home from work early that day with devastating news. He had lost his job after being deemed a liability due to a neurological condition that caused seizures. His driver's license was revoked too. He showed no other physical symptoms. What caused it? I didn't want to believe it!

Shocked by the news, it felt like someone had sucker punched me in the stomach. I couldn't breathe. Why was this happening? We were already amid a challenging court battle with the bank to save our home. Now this? I became an emotional wreck, consumed with negative thoughts: Anthony's disabled and unemployed, I'm not working, we have no income, my family is homeless...

Feeling helpless, I drowned in my emotions. It was getting the best of me. I began allowing worry, anxiety, anger, and fear to consume me. I was physically weak from all the sleepless nights, thoughts of shame and embarrassment, and fear of becoming homeless and broke. What would others think? I was angry. Why us? I felt like I was losing my mind! I was emotionally exhausted, and I just wanted to give up.

Caught up in my emotions, I forgot to invite God's presence, power, protection, provision, and peace. When I finally paused and caught my breath, I was reminded of the scripture, "Why are ye fearful, O ye of little faith?" (Matthew 8:26 KJV). I was focused on the circumstances, and I magnified them, forgetting the power of prayer.

"Be anxious for nothing, but in everything by prayer and supplication, with thanksgiving, let your requests be made known to God; and the peace of God, which surpasses all understanding, will guard your hearts and minds through Christ Jesus" (Philippians 4:6-7 NKJV). As I prayed, I felt the Holy Spirit empowering and strengthening me, shifting my thoughts to God's promises, which were stored in my heart. He was aligning my heart with my mind and guiding me to focus on Him.

I could hear, "You belong to me. I love you. I am your Heavenly Father. You are My daughter." He told me, "Worry, anxiety, anger, and fear are not of Me!"

As I prayed, I was reminded of who God had been in my life and how he had answered many of my other prayers. He is my miracle worker, way-maker, and promise-keeper, and nothing is impossible for Him. Faith began rising in my spirit! He stirred up the "mustard seed" faith He had given me, hallelujah!

So began the process of "exercising," stretching my faith "muscles." My first exercise: trust and believe the promises my Heavenly Father spoke to me. His promises activated my faith. Next, pray and ask with thanksgiving. As I continued to exercise my faith, my prayers grew fervent. They were bold, with a confident expectancy that He would answer. I continued praying for Anthony's healing, a financial breakthrough, protection over our home, patience, and peace. Our church family was interceding for us, and so was Jesus! I was praying for a miracle.

I felt like the woman in the Bible who kept going back to court, pleading her case to an unjust judge until he finally gave her what she wanted (Luke 18:1-8 KJV). My mind and heart were aligning with His promises, trusting, and believing Him, leaning on Him. He was in control. My emotions, my feelings, no longer ruled over me.

I would speak to myself, "My Heavenly Father loves me, and His perfect love casts out all my fears" (1 John 4:18 KJV). As my faith increased, my desire was to please my Heavenly Father. My focus was no longer on what I prayed for, but to whom I was praying. Almighty God, my Heavenly Father! Praising Him, giving Him thanks for who He is, I felt the Lord's love pour over me and in me, comforting me, embracing me like a young child against her mother's bosom. I saw Him as my security "blanket." He opened my spiritual eyes to see Him. That was the miracle.

Every time I think of that moment, tears well up in my eyes. God is so, so good! I never imagined that was the actual miracle I was praying for. But the Holy Spirit knew. He interceded on my behalf for the miracle, opening my spiritual eyes. "For we walk by faith, not by sight" (2 Corinthians 5:7 KJV). Hope rose in me, a confident expectancy that God would answer my prayer.

So, did He? Has He answered your prayers? Do you recall how excited and grateful you were when He answered? I'm so overwhelmed with gratitude and His faithfulness as I share this. In 2013, three years after Anthony lost his job, finally, a financial breakthrough. Anthony's Social Security disability claim was approved. He was awarded a lump-sum check, which provided the necessary funds to get back on our feet, and his entitled monthly Social Security disability income. In addition, he received another lump-sum check from long-term disability insurance. Double-portion blessings!

In 2015, we were able to repurchase our home, which Anthony and our sons had built, for more than $100K lower than the original cost. We gained more than $50K in equity, and our mortgage payment was cut in half. Double-portion blessings!

Twelve years later, God healed Anthony of the seizures, and his driver's license was restored. Looking back, I can see God had a big plan for our home. Returning our home back to us was significant because two families were at risk of becoming homeless. My daughter and her family were living with us at the time. Later, He also provided a home for other members of our family. My son, daughter-in-law, and their young daughter moved into our home, as his wife was pregnant with twins. Another double-portion blessing! However, the youngest twin was born with a life-threatening condition. Her little lungs were underdeveloped, and she struggled to breathe. The doctors did everything medically possible for her...she was in God's hands.

The family gathered in the hospital chapel, and we were all devastated at the thought of losing her. We prayed for a miracle. I was blessed to be one of the few family members allowed in the NICU to witness her dedication to the Lord. We watched in amazement as her eyes opened at the mention of Jesus' name. I saw the spirit of the Lord in her, His spirit strengthened her fragile little body and filled her with life. She became alert, her color changed, and her stats improved. The medical staff was in awe. Imagine the excitement and joy of witnessing this miracle. Another answered prayer!

Four years later, our princess warrior's journey has not been easy. She depends on a ventilator to support her breathing but is thriving in our home with love and support from her family. We continue praying for her healing and look forward to the day she will be completely healed, healthy, and whole. She is a precious child of God. He created and named her for a purpose. He named her Faith. As I see her each day, she is my constant reminder of His faithfulness. Faith is part of my faith walk. I am blessed to see how the Lord in her inspires so many people.

So, did my Heavenly Father answer the rest of my prayer for patience and peace? He's faithful, right? He answered, but not the way I imagined He would. He used the challenges and difficulties I faced to draw me closer to Him and experience spiritual growth in my relationship with Him. It was an opportunity for me to release my faith, to see that His plan for me was for good, to build trust, and receive His peace. Through the difficulties, He was with me, holding my hand as His Holy Spirit guided and comforted me and taught me to persevere, which produced patience. He taught me time is my trainer. Imagine praying, waiting, and trusting for twelve years for Anthony's healing to be manifested! I learned that answered prayers come on His timetable, not mine.

Life's challenges are God setting a scene for His intervention. When difficulties arise in my life, Jesus lifts me higher and reminds me to whom I belong. I pray you remember who you belong to too. From faith to faith, my journey continues...Glory to God!

About the Author

First-time author Isabelle Ramos contributed to an anthology, *Women with Unshakeable Faith*, releasing April 23, 2023.

At a young age, Isabelle discovered her love for sketching and sewing. Embracing her creative gift, she studied fashion and interior design. After thirty years of fashion merchandising, management, display, and interior design, she opened a gift/antique shop, promoting other local artists.

She served eight years in children's ministry, teaching "The Fruit of the Spirit," etiquette, and Sunday Bible classes. She is a prayer warrior, loves spending devotional time with Jesus, and fellowshipping/sharing with her "sisters." She enjoys fun time with her grand-girls, baking, being creative, doing arts and crafts, and sharing the joy of knowing Jesus!

She resides in Suisun City, California, with Anthony, her husband of fifty years. They have four children, ten grandchildren, and one great-grandchild.

Connect with Isabelle

- Email: Inspired1000@gmail.com

- IG: www.Instagram.com/passion4healthwealth

- Facebook: www.facebook.com/IsabelleRamos

The Fight for My Life

Jackie Mungo

The doctor walked in and said, "How old did you say you were?"

I looked at him and asked, "Do I have cancer?"

"Yes, you do."

Everything became a blur, tears streamed down my face, and I could barely hear anything he said after that. Grateful that my mother was with me, the doctor told me my options. "You can have a lumpectomy, which is the removal of the lump, or you can have a mastectomy, which is the removal of your breast. If we perform a lumpectomy, you may have to have chemotherapy or radiation, but if you have a mastectomy, you may not."

It was so much to take in. I was newly divorced, my daughter and I were on our own, and now this. What was I going to do? At that time, when you heard the word "cancer," you immediately thought about death or grave illness because of treatment. I decided at that moment no one else was going to raise my daughter. I was going to fight!

I never thought the lump I had found months previously in my breast would be cancer. When I first felt the lump, I went to the doctor immediately and was told it was nothing, I was young, and to come back in three months. Three months later, I returned only to hear the same thing, but the doctor said he would measure it. During this time, I changed medical plans and went to a new doctor for a routine checkup and told him about the lump. He said, "Did you have a mammogram?"

I said no, and he started the ball rolling. I got a mammogram and an ultrasound. Since I was so young, it was hard to see if anything was suspicious on a mammogram. The ultrasound showed it was indeed cancer. The doctor asked, "How old did you say you were?" I was only twenty-seven. Cancer was devastating news for a young mother. What was I going to do?

Fight!

The following week I had a mastectomy. My mother informed my family. For some reason, I couldn't speak about the diagnosis. The calls from friends and family began pouring in, and the love was real. Support came from coworkers and my church family as well. Even hospital administrators came to visit me since I was one of the youngest ladies in the Bay Area to be diagnosed with breast cancer at that time. And even with a cancer diagnosis, I had the Lord's favor. All the support was overwhelming but so appreciated. If it wasn't for the outpouring of love, I don't know how I would have gotten through that time.

After my surgery, I received a call from an American Cancer Society volunteer, who offered to visit me, share her story, and bring me information about what I was going through along with a temporary prosthesis. That volunteer made a huge impact on me. Speaking to someone who had gone through it helped me feel like I was not alone. All that, along with my faith in God and a positive attitude, got me through the trial.

Six months after the mastectomy, I had breast reconstruction, which is called a TRAM flap. They take fat from your stomach and make a breast with it, so you get a tummy tuck as well. When I share my story, I always say I got a new rack and flat stomach out of the deal. Always look on the bright side.

That volunteer inspired me to volunteer and help women braving the same diagnosis. This allowed me to share my story and give those women hope that they could make it after a diagnosis of cancer. The American Cancer Society called on me to share my story to inspire women to get mammograms and stay on top of their health.

Two years after my diagnosis, I started working for the American Cancer Society. My first position was as a secretary. God put my foot in the door before I had even realized it. By volunteering and sharing my story, they knew me and welcomed me into the organization. I became their poster child. I was literally on posters, pamphlets, and videos telling my story of survivorship, sharing that cancer is not a death sentence and that there is hope. I became an advocate and still am to this day. My family became involved by volunteering and sharing the message of hope with their friends. There are commercials and pamphlets out there with my brother, niece, and cousins on them.

I worked my way up from secretary to the director of my own office in Richmond, California, where I managed volunteers and a board of directors for West Contra Costa. The American Cancer Society employed me for exactly twenty years to the day, only ending the relationship because of budget cuts throughout the organization. During my tenure at the American Cancer Society, I met some wonderful people and am still friends with them to this day. I also met my husband, Rochon Mungo Sr., a UPS driver who worked in the same area I worked, which was another divine connection. Working for the American Cancer Society also prepared me to be a caregiver, which you will hear about in my next book, so stay tuned.

Having cancer matured me and made me who I am today. Several local television stations interviewed me, my story was featured in *Ebony* and *Heart and Soul* magazines, and I graced the cover of calendars, which highlighted cancer survivors and their stories. I say this not to brag or boast but to show how a cancer diagnosis is not the end-all. For a while, I struggled whenever my diagnosis anniversary came up. I feared it would come back. But my pastor gave me some scripture, and I have held onto it and shared it with the diagnosed women I speak to: "What do ye imagine against the Lord? He will make an utter end: affliction shall not rise up the second time" (Nahum 1:9 KJV).

My fight with cancer was about getting me to who I am and who I am called to be. I am an advocate for those who do not have voices. I am an example of hope after a cancer diagnosis and a place you can turn to.

The Healing Institute Global Network was born out of my experience with cancer and being a caregiver to my husband, who also had cancer. My mantra is, "No one should face cancer alone." So the Healing Institute Global Network offers support not only to cancer survivors but their families as well. We offer rides to treatments and emotional support to all. We have successfully coordinated two cancer walks honoring cancer survivors, thrivers, victors, and warriors. We have held three fashion shows highlighting survivors and what being healed from cancer looks like. If you or someone you know has been touched by cancer and needs support or someone to talk to, please contact The Healing Institute Global Network at or 510-394-5447.

I am grateful to God for this cancer journey and where it continues taking me. I am in awe of what the Lord has done, and He never ceases to amaze me with new journeys and new opportunities. My family used to tease me about doing so much cancer advocacy in the community, saying that one day I would be on *Oprah*. It's not too late, family. I still have that out there.

Thirty-two years later, I'm still fighting. I'm not fighting for myself but fighting for others who are battling this disease. Speak the Word over yourself constantly and be healed.

"Heal me, O Lord, and I shall be healed" (Jeremiah 17:14 KJV). Believe it! Receive it!

About the Author

First-time author Jackie Mungo co-authored an anthology, *Women with Unshakeable Faith.* Jackie is a thirty-plus-year breast cancer survivor and was a loving and devoted caregiver to her husband, Rochon Mungo, Sr. Jackie is the founder/CEO of The Healing Institute Global Network based in Oakland, California. Among her many accomplishments, she was featured in *Ebony* magazine and had numerous national television appearances advocating for cancer patients and their families. She holds that her life's calling is to serve, which she considers a labor of love. Jackie knows that a book has been in her mind and heart for many years. She is intentional about service to her community, and she is a twenty-four-hour, seven-day-a-week advocate for those fighting cancer.

Connect with Jackie:

- Website: www.thehealinginstitute.org
- Facebook: The Healing Institute Global Network
- IG: Jackie Mungo (@thehealinginstituteglobal)
- Website: jackiemungo.com

No More Secrets

Jennifer M. Jackson

"Regardless, if they can't get past the introduction of your story, don't allow the opinions of others to be the pen that edits God's purpose for your life. Remember, it's His ink that will always last!"

Think back to a time in your childhood when your closest friend said, "If I tell you a secret, will you keep it just between you and me?" Did you look at your friend in dismay, thinking, when did you ever reveal something to me and later it was posted for all the world to see? Look at the adult you are and realize you aren't a child anymore. Now you're ready to tell the whole world your secret. Deep breathe...here we go.

I held on to that secret for the past forty-one years. Yep, you read it right, no typos or misspellings. For forty-one years I held on to the secret that I was molested by a family member.

Coming into 2022, God was already helping me forgive and release people so I could move forward into my purpose and destiny. The first person, of all people, was the one who molested me. In my mind, I went back and forth with the Lord, sarcastically saying, "You for real, right?"

His response to me was simply, "Yes." So, being obedient, I mustered up the strength to reach out to that man via text. I told him I forgave him for what he did to me.

Of course, his response was, *I don't know what you think you need to forgive me for.*

I didn't respond. I wasn't going to throw away the peace and freedom God had given me.

The final person I needed to reveal this secret to was my biological mother. I toiled with the decision so hard, then I reached out to a family member whom I have a good relationship with. At the end of the conversation, I just said, "All my life I have been carrying this secret and protecting others. What about me?"

Just this past November 2022, God gave me peace and said, "Now is the time."

So, I spoke with my mother. I said, "Please don't hate this person. I am not coming to you now with this, but I need to tell you my truth."

"I didn't know, and I am so sorry this happened." Her apology gave me peace, and I was released and freed from this secret. It felt like losing twenty pounds.

During this processing and healing, God had me send that man a card wishing him the best. When God wants you healed and delivered, He will do things like that.

What did forty-one years of holding on to this secret cost me? Or better yet, where did it take me?

We have heard about the spirit of offense. I even read John Bereve's *The Bait of Satan*, and not even that book could have prepared me for what I know is a bitter judgment or root of bitterness until the beginning of 2022. "Looking diligently lest any man fail of the grace of God; lest any root of bitterness springing up trouble you, and thereby many be defiled" (Hebrews 12:15 KJV).

God showed me in many ways this seed had been planted, and it still had life because I was holding on to the secret. Each day you willfully hold on, you are giving life to what needs to be uprooted. I thought I was good to go with God. He was like, "Yeah right Jennifer, you need to get out of My way and let Me *be* the way." I wasn't about to argue with Him.

As you read this, you may be thinking, who in their right mind would hold on to a secret for forty-one years? What were you thinking holding on to this secret for so long? Well, I am so glad you asked that question. I was four years old when this happened. I was in foster care, and I didn't want to be removed from the home if I told what had happened to me during a home visit with my biological mother. Even now, as an adult, I know it was nothing but the grace and mercy of God that I was able to hold on to this secret, thinking it was for others' good when all the while it tore me up.

Only through the mighty will and grace of God was I able to manage and function. I fell into cycles of depression and low self-esteem, where I became a functioning depressant. I developed a love-hate relationship with food, and not even a gym membership could help me work this secret off. I battled with suicidal thoughts my entire life. Blaming God, I said, "If only you wouldn't have allowed me to be born, this would have never happened."

Holding on to this secret unbalanced my emotions, and I warily determined how close both males and females could get to me. I almost dared people to ask me about my life, only to shut them down. This past fall, when I was talking to a friend at the gym, God said it so clearly but softly, "You have an offense against black men." I cried, not caring who saw me, and repented as He showed me. "I don't need you to function, I need you to live. Yes, this is where the hurt started, but that's no longer your truth. You can't hold someone else accountable for that person's actions." Let me tell you, that weight was gone and out the door.

My healing process and being delivered from this secret all started back in 2020 with one of my Army jobs. I am a sexual assault response coordinator (SARC). I am an advocate, and I also do training for my organization. A training video entitled *Voiceless* consisted of five different gentlemen telling their stories, and the second story mirrored mine in so many ways. I had to watch this video ten times. I found myself getting up from my desk trying to avoid watching it, let alone having to give the training.

On the tenth time, God stopped me and reminded me, "You are stronger than you think. This is no longer your story, but someone needs to hear it. I got you." Peace came over me. I completed the training and had no issues sharing my story. Now I share it when led to.

If it wasn't for my faith in God, my relationship with Jesus and the Holy Spirit, there wouldn't have been a way for me to walk this out by faith. God reminded me through this process His presence is forever there. "Let your conversation be without covetousness; and be content with such things as ye have: for he hath said, I will never leave thee, nor forsake thee" (Hebrews 13:5 KJV).

God reminded me that He placed me in a position to help others, and I couldn't walk into my next season of coaching and mentoring and expect honesty if I wasn't being honest with the person I was called to help, or even myself. Maybe you or someone you know are struggling with a secret. God will always make a way. The love He has for you is greater than any secret keeping you bound. He is your strength. You are more powerful than you know. Your season of secrets is closed.

Just know that whatever decision you make today, I decree and declare over your life that every dark secret, every form of hurt, rejection, the spirit of suicide, the spirit of self-doubt, those generational things are broken off your life and generations to come. I decree and declare that the power of healing and deliverance rests upon you. The spirit of unforgiveness no longer binds you. You are walking in the power of your purpose and whom God has called and mandated you to be before the foundation of the world. Amen!

About the Author

Jennifer M. Jackson is the author of *It Didn't Break Me: My Personal Struggle with Depression and How One Word from God Changed My Life* and *You Can't Afford To Go Back: It's Time To Cross Over* and co-author of *It Cost Me Everything* and her latest anthology, *Women with Unshakable Faith*, where she shares how she overcame the secret of being molested by a family member and allowed the power of forgiveness to propel her toward her purpose with passion and perseverance. She is an active-duty service member who serves as a sexual assault response coordinator (SARC) for the United States Army. She also serves as a court-appointed special advocate for the state of Louisiana, where she advocates for children in foster care.

Connect with Jennifer

- Instagram: https://instagram.com/jennifermjackson_
- Website: www.nomoresecrets.me

ALIVE TO TESTIFY

Donna Yates

Building Blocks to My Souled-Out Faith

"As you go through the peaks and valleys of life, let God's peace be your guide."

As I think back on my journey to developing souled-out faith, I realize that God's peace has been my constant companion. My faith and trust in God during each pivotal moment released His peace. At those very moments, He was at work. The presence of peace didn't change those situations, but the Holy Spirit changed the atmosphere. He changed the way I viewed the situations and provided presence of mind. He is our very present help! I didn't know where He was taking me, nor did I know the outcome. But I did know He was handling each situation. "For we walk by faith, not by sight" (2 Corinthians 5:7 KJV). I am grateful to be alive to testify about His goodness and all He has done in my life. Each experience has been a building block to increase my faith.

You can't rely on others' faith: "That your faith should not stand in the wisdom of men, but in the power of God" (1 Corinthians 2:5 KJV). Early in my faith, I looked up to my mentors. I clung to their every word and relied on their faith. They could get a prayer through to God. It felt like they had Jesus on speed dial, and He answered on the first ring. I, on the other hand, felt like my name and number were blocked, and I was on the do-not-disturb list. My prayers went up but were rejected as soon as they left my mouth. The reason: lack of faith. "But without faith it's impossible to please him" (Hebrews 11:6 KJV). I had a relationship with God but not an intimate one.

On my thirty-third birthday, I heard God's voice so clearly, I looked around to see if anyone else heard Him. I was there with my mentors, friends, and mother. During the celebration, God said, "You will not be with your church sisters like this again."

"Really, Lord?" I either saw each sister or we spoke on the telephone daily. Despite the message, I was calm and at peace. But since that day, we have not been together again.

I learned three very important things: God was talking to me, He meant what He said, and He wanted me to get off the spiritual bottle and begin to eat the meat of His Word for myself. My faith needed to increase without interference from those I spiritually looked up to. Their faith wouldn't get me through the peaks or valleys of my life. Only He could bring me through. This experience was one of the first building blocks that would increase my faith. As I got closer to God, I realized I had never been on the do-not-disturb list. I had been calling the wrong number.

Don't walk through the valley of the shadow of death alone. My mother, Wanna Wright, was larger than life in my eyes. She appeared to be invincible. At age twenty-eight, she had already had a full hysterectomy. Right after hearing about Minnie Riperton's death, she found a lump and was diagnosed with breast cancer at age thirty-two. By thirty-three, she had a radical mastectomy. It's hard to imagine being in the prime of your life, married with three teenagers, unable to bear additional children, and losing your breasts. Thank God she survived.

Because she was alive to testify, she made it her life's mission to educate other women and men in early detection. She advocated, ensuring the underserved could get free exams. She even self-published a book of poems and a spoken-word CD to share her story, entitled *Alive to Testify*.

I was thirteen at the time of her diagnosis and mastectomy. During almost all of my teen years and into adulthood, I was concerned about being diagnosed with breast cancer. It was a nagging thought I just couldn't shake. I made sure my doctors knew how young my mom was when diagnosed and that my maternal grandmother had breast cancer as well. She had died so young I couldn't ask her any questions about her journey.

My mother taught me how and when to do self-exams and what to look out for. I started getting mammograms at age thirty-three, and doctors suggested I have a mammogram every two years. I needed to watch like a hawk for any abnormalities in my breasts.

In 2007, we had begun a new life in our new home. I started over with new doctors and was scheduled for my annual mammogram. While in the examination room, the technician took the images, then another person reviewed them. Did she see something? The silence was piercing. She said the doctor would get back to me if she had any questions. To my surprise, the doctor called the same day. She wanted to see me in her office to conduct an exam.

While in her office, she confirmed what the technician saw on the image. She felt the lump. It was about the size of a pea. I had missed it completely while conducting my self-examinations. Everything she said after that sounded like white noise, like an out-of-body experience. Once the doctor placed my finger on the area, I could feel it. It was there! How did I miss it? I was thinking, why am I here alone? This can't be happening. I whispered, "God help me!" And there it was. An overwhelming feeling of peace settled over me despite the possible life-or-death situation. It was like God was telling me not to worry and that everything would be okay. He was the help I needed at that very moment. Worrying would not change anything. I had faith that God would see me through. My next task was to break the news to my mom and my husband. I thought, Lord, give me the courage.

Though I worried all those years about a breast cancer diagnosis, it was Mom's worst fear. As I shared the news with her, she remained silent, though she was never at a loss for words. Once I told her that I was at peace regarding the news, she breathed a sigh of relief. She insisted on going through every step with my husband and me. On the day of my biopsy, I was calm. I felt God's love covering me. But getting the results back felt like an eternity.

It was benign! Praise the Lord. We all celebrated, though my mother only celebrated for two seconds and then insisted I get a second opinion, so I did. My doctor and a surgeon at Stanford suggested I have the tumor removed. They didn't think it wise to leave it there and watch it. We all agreed.

It's been almost sixteen years since my scare, and God has kept me. We've lost friends and family members along the way to this terrible disease. I don't have those nagging thoughts anymore, but I'm fully aware of the importance of breast self-exams and annual mammograms, as we all should.

I share these pivotal moments in my life to remind you that you are not alone. We all go through peaks and valleys. God doesn't promise a problem-free life, but He does promise to be with us through it all. Becoming a woman of unshakeable faith requires going through, coming through, and remembering the goodness of God and how He brought us through. Each experience should increase our faith.

Here are a few of the action steps that helped me strengthen my faith.

Action 1: Read your Bible and pray daily. Be specific when you pray. Get a Bible translation that helps the Word come alive in you.

Action 2: Purchase a journal. Make an appointment with the Lord every day and keep it. Get quiet and listen. Ask God questions and record the Holy Spirit's responses.

Action 3: Begin your day with a heart full of thankfulness and gratitude. Record your thoughts. It will encourage your faith for the next peak or valley you face.

Action 4: Purchase a dream journal and place it by your bed. Upon waking from your dreams, immediately capture the details. Pray for the interpretation.

Action 5: Ask God to let your light shine so that others can see Him through you. Be ready to respond when they say they see the glory of the Lord in you.

Action 6: Join other like-minded believers, such as the Voices of Healing prayer line every Saturday at eight a.m. PST (605-313-5111 Pin 345952#).

I'm grateful to be alive to testify of His goodness. The experiences He brought me through were building blocks to increase, encourage, and strengthen my faith. I am souled out for Jesus and am grateful to have unshakeable faith.

About the Author

Two-time best-selling author Donna Yates recently co-authored an anthology, *Women with Unshakeable Faith*, releasing in April 2023. She also co-authored *Resilience in Hard Times* and *When Queen's Rise*.

Through her passion for writing, a love for the Lord, and music, Donna co-wrote a children's gospel CD entitled *Souled Out*. The CD entitled song, "Souled Out," was performed on the legendary *Showtime at the Apollo*.

She graduated from San Jose State University with a Bachelor of Arts in Economics and Marketing. She recently graduated to become a chaplain.

Donna is a businesswoman and desires to empower and equip other businesswomen. Her "Voices of Healing" prayer call was established in 2017 as a source of support for other businesswomen to pray together.

Donna resides in Fairfield, California, with her husband Joseph. She is the mother of two and the yaya of eight.

Connect with Donna:

- Email: Donnyates30@gmail.com
- Facebook: https://www.facebook.com/donna.yates.71619
- Instagram: 1blessedyayapapaWebsite: donnayates.com

GOD SAID, "I'M NOT FINISHED WITH YOU YET"

JANAY THOMPSON

"Do not date anyone for the remainder of 2019."

I responded desperately, "But he is everything I prayed for in a man!"

In the stillest of voices, the Lord reiterated, "Do not date anyone for the remainder of 2019." In my spirit, being obedient was a no-brainer, but in my heart, the struggle was real. Left to decide my next move, I chose to go against God's direction and follow my own path. Somebody cue the *Family Feud* buzzer because that was the wrong answer. What "felt" right in my heart turned out to be nearly fatal to my faith. It was also the catalyst for a series of events that almost ended my life.

Some may wonder how I heard God so vividly yet blatantly ignored His warning. Frankly, dating was my comfort zone, no matter the level of toxicity. And comfortable was the only way I wanted to live.

Being alone was agonizing, and I didn't like myself enough to be alone for long. Doing life on my terms was a blaring red flag that my faith was far removed from the Lord. Don't get me wrong, by 2019, I had been through enough trials to learn to trust God, but only with a few things, such as my finances, career opportunities, school endeavors, and His ability to help me find a good parking spot at the supermarket. But to trust Him to mend my broken heart from past relationships, deliver me from the spirit of fear and loneliness, and give me the grace to confidently walk in a season of singleness, not so much. So, I gave God a hard no and continued doing my own thing. And just as quickly as I disregarded Him, I realized why I should have listened.

It was January 7, 2020, the day my world changed forever. I closed myself in the bathroom of my little one-bedroom apartment, the same place God had given me the warning. I prayed with my eyes shut tightly. After the allotted three minutes of waiting, the results were in. I hesitantly opened my eyes, and there it was: a positive pregnancy test. I wept silently, then emerged from my bathroom and showed my boyfriend the test. With a nervous smile, he assured me everything would be okay, even though we both knew that "okay" was subjective given the circumstances. He and I had just met in August 2019, and we barely knew each other's middle names.

The months following felt like I was in a virtual reality world; I could see everything in front of me, but nothing felt real. I prayed, begging God to remove me from my body, to take me out of my misery, or at least take the baby out of my womb so I could evade the consequences of my actions. I even began planning for an abortion, but once I realized I was scheduling the appointment on my birthday, I understood abortion was not an option for me. How could I celebrate another year of my life while actively planning to take the life of my unborn child? I felt miserable throughout my entire pregnancy, and it wasn't morning sickness.

My boyfriend and I fought nearly every day about everything. What once felt like a dream come true turned out to be one of the hardest relationships I had ever been in. I asked God, "Why are you allowing my life to be in such disarray?"

He told me, "End the relationship, and trust Me to give you the love and peace you desperately long for."

My response was no, again. The relationship's dysfunction felt safer than the unknown result of trusting God with my life. I refused to put my faith in Him to carry my heart. I wanted to be in control, even if it meant living in dysfunction.

Once our son arrived, things were peaceful for some time, and I finally saw the light at the end of the tunnel. The pandemic, although terrifying at times, provided an opportunity for us to enjoy our baby with few visitors. And while I quite enjoyed the solitude, the enemy used the isolation to attack my mind. A few weeks after my son's birth, I slipped into postpartum depression. Anxiety filled my mind and clouded my judgment. I picked fights with my boyfriend, mother, sisters, boss, and anyone else who dared to challenge me. The inevitable eventuated. My boyfriend insisted we break up, and since I couldn't force him to stay and continue being a crutch for my fear of loneliness, I obliged. My life spiraled out of control, and everything I feared happening, happened. Have you ever been there?

Despondent and broken, I tried to continue a normal life, until one day, I couldn't take the pain anymore. Since my baby was with his grandmother, it was the perfect moment for me to succumb to my mental demise. I grabbed my ex-boyfriend's gun and one of my baby's onesies and headed to my favorite place in Memphis, the Mississippi River view at Harbor Town. After parking in an isolated area, I gripped my baby's shirt and stared at the river in front of me. Tears welled in my eyes as fear, guilt, and shame overwhelmed my mind. "You're not only worthless, but you're selfish too. Your baby deserves better than you. Go ahead, get on with it. Everyone will be better off." The enemy was having a field day with my mind.

I cried, "God, I can't do this anymore! Please, help me!" I picked up the gun, loaded with one bullet.

Then God said, "I am not finished with you yet." It was the same small voice I had heard back in 2019. Truthfully, I knew ending my life was not the answer. I just wanted to take the pain away and feel seen again. At that moment, at the river, when all hope was gone, I felt seen. I wasn't saved by some knight in shining armor, nor had anything changed in my circumstances. The voice of God grabbed me off the ledge, and I was overcome by immense love. There was nothing left to do but worship the Lord; so I worshipped.

After I gathered my bearings, I headed home to relish in the euphoria of being in the loving presence of the almighty God. I had not anticipated returning home not only alive but with a newfound hope in Christ Jesus. I returned to God's original instruction and spent the next few months intentionally alone to cultivate my relationship with Christ. I fasted and removed everything and everyone from my life that did not serve me or the God in me. I became baptized in the Holy Spirit and began studying His word like never before. With Jesus as my guiding light, I knew that, no matter what happened to me from that point forward, I could not fail. I had finally become full of the fruits of the spirit. I was made whole.

Time passed, and the Lord decided to mend my relationship with my ex. As we dated His way, with no sin or immorality attached to our relationship, God made all things new just as He promised. He perfected that which concerned us, and my boyfriend was led to accept Christ as his Lord and Savior too. My boyfriend didn't accept Christ for me, my expression of faith gave room for God to turn his heart of stone into a heart of flesh. The next year, we made a covenant with God, got married, and became pregnant with our second son. Once I delighted myself in the Lord, He gave me my heart's desires, and then some! Ain't He alright?

"There is no fear in love; but perfect love casts out fear, because fear involves torment. But he who fears has not been made perfect in love" (1 John 4:18 NKJV). A few verses prior to this, we are reminded that God is love. Since God is love, those who are in Him cannot also be in fear. It is not God's desire that any of us should perish. He wants us all to have life more abundantly. Apart from Him, I was nothing, and I had nothing; but with Him, I became a victorious woman with unshakable faith. Glory be to the Most High God!

About the Author

First-time author Janay Thompson has contributed to the anthology *Women with Unshakable Faith*, releasing in April 2023.

As a wife and mother of two, Janay has an exuberant passion for faith and family. With a bachelor's degree in child development and family studies, she strives to become an advocate for Christian families, emphasizing the importance of God's design for the family structure.

Born and raised in Memphis, Tennessee, Janay is a dynamic leader, serving as a Sunday school teacher and a worship leader at her church, a baby prep mentor at Life Choices in Memphis, and a social counselor at Tennessee Early Intervention System. She enjoys dancing, singing, cooking, and spending time with her husband, children, and family. Janay hopes that through her life, people can feel the love of God and be led to know Christ in a deeper, more meaningful way.

Connect with Janay

- JanayBThompson@gmail.com

- https://www.instagram.com/_naybre/

- https://www.facebook.com/janay.clark2?mibextid=LQQJ4d

- https://janaybthompson.my.canva.site/

Faith to Believe

Ebone' Marie

"God is a God of details, every piece of the puzzle is important to produce the whole picture." -Ebone' Marie

I knew he was the one, until he wasn't. Then I shut down and closed myself off until I was ready. The next time would be different. Then I finally met the one I would spend forever with. But forever fell short a few years and became never. At that point, I began questioning if I would ever be someone's wife. Always the bridesmaid, never the bride, or sometimes not even part of her tribe. I began to think God forgot about me. Have you ever felt that way? Like God was taking care of everyone around you and leaving you hanging. What if I told you there was more to the story than what you were feeling, seeing, or experiencing at that moment? Well, there is more to the story.

When I was a little girl, I dreamed of getting married at the church I grew up in and wearing a beautiful gown with a train covering the whole aisle. I thought it would be just like the television show *Boy Meets World*. I would marry my high school sweetheart. You know, that Cory and Topanga type of love. We'd get married after college, have 3 ½ kids by thirty years old, and live in a beautiful house with a dog. Life would be perfect. In reality, when I turned thirty, I was in an uncommitted, it's-complicated, he's-the-one, but-he's-not, here-we-go-again situationship. Have you had one of those? One word: toxic.

Let me take you back to the beginning. We met unexpectedly on vacation, and it seemed perfect. We had great chemistry and constant communication, and we worked to build a good friendship. He seemed to just understand me. When we were together, it felt like we were the only ones in the room. This was what I had dreamed of. This was what I had waited for! He had to be the one I had seen in my dreams because everything seemed perfect. Until, one day, it wasn't. I'm still not sure what happened, but it broke me and my heart. The constant communication stopped. Then, with no explanation, he would reach out to me and act as if nothing happened. I grew bitter toward him and cautious with other men. I put too much trust in him and our relationship for it to end the way it did. Yet I was still hopeful, and over the next few years, I would open myself up to him then close him out again in a continuous cycle.

I finally tired of the back and forth. It happened when we were rebuilding our situationship, and he made a decision that caused me to lose trust in him again. It was then that I cried out to God. "Why does this keep happening? Why do I continue going through this cycle with him? You told me I would be married. Why am I not married yet? I saw in my dreams that I would be married and have kids. You showed it to me! Why hasn't it happened?" At that moment, I realized I was missing something. What it was, I wasn't completely sure. However, I knew what I had to do: completely surrender myself to God.

One of my favorite scriptures is Psalm 37:4 (NKJV), "Delight yourself also in the Lord, And He shall give you the desires of your heart." When I studied this scripture, I recognized that just going to church and serving wasn't enough. God wanted a relationship with me. My situationship mimicked my relationship with God. I was back and forth with God but expected Him to bless me with a husband. How could I be a good wife if I couldn't steward a proper relationship with God? I wanted to be married because that was the next part of life, at least that's what the world said. I also wanted to feed my fleshly desires. God desires more from marriage; it is a kingdom covenant He wants and will bless.

As I began reading the Bible, studying His word, praying, and meditating, my relationship with God grew, and my desire for marriage changed. I no longer wanted to be married just to be married, I want a kingdom covenant marriage that would do great works for God's kingdom. God gave me the desire to be married, but I hadn't sought His word or Him to understand why. When I experienced a revelation of why He wanted me married, I began allowing Him to heal me so I could walk in my purpose. As I did this, I thought for sure I would be married right away. I was wrong.

Here I am almost forty years old, and I'm still not married. I don't even have any prospects. The only thing I have from my plans as a little girl is my dog. Instead of complaining, I asked God, "What am I missing?"

He told me, "I am giving you your heart's desire." There is one desire of utmost importance to me that I barely speak of to others, but

I have fervently prayed for: to have my biological father walk me down the aisle. My mother passed away when I was five years old, and I was raised by my dad's mother. Due to his life journey, he wasn't around consistently. I got used to him not being around and had other people in mind who could walk me down the aisle, but my heart's desire was always for him to be by my side. A small detail in the big picture, but God is working it out just for me. Or shall I say, He is working it out for us. My dad's journey is improving, and we are building our relationship, so I can truly have the wedding of my dreams.

I know what God is doing isn't just for me, it's also for my family and those who will witness the beauty of God turning things around. I may not be married or have any prospects, yet, but this is bigger than me. Our lives are bigger than just us; they are for those we encounter to help change their lives as well.

I encourage you to have faith in what God promises you. Every moment is just as important as the next, no matter how big or small. God is in the details of our stories, and we must have faith and know it will all come in His perfect timing. I have faith I will be married and have a beautiful family, and my biological father will walk me down the aisle. I also have faith in God's promises to you.

"Now faith is the substance of things hoped for, the evidence of things not seen" (Hebrews 11:1 NKJV).

About the Author

Author Ebone' Marie released her first book, *The Beauty Within Let the Journey Begin*, in May 2022, and co-authored an anthology, *Women with Unshakeable Faith*, to be released in April 2023. Ebone' Marie is the former podcast host of *Love Thyself* featured on Vercay Radio, which was birthed from her journey of learning to love and see herself as God does. Her heart is to see women be healed from past traumas, heartaches, heartbreaks, disappointments, and failures from their pasts, and live a life of wholeness fulfilling their purpose. Ebone' Marie uses her life's testimonies to help others realize God's love for them and their potential to live a love-filled, purposeful life.

Connect with Ebone'

- Facebook: https://www.facebook.com/lovethyself18
- IG: @theebonemarie

Ten Days at the Feet of God

Chapri Johnson

"For I know the plans I have for you saith the Lord, thoughts of peace and not of evil to bring you to an expected end." Jeremiah 29: 11 KJV

What does stress look like to you? More importantly, how do you handle it when it comes knocking at your door? Let me just say, "Stress will come. It's unrealistic to think we won't face it. As mothers we juggle life, family, and work (whether outside the home or inside) with some level of stress during the day. What happens when there are multiple chronic stressors occurring simultaneously, what do you do? You sit up, stop what you're doing, and you pay attention! Nothing would prepare me for the terror that would unfold in January of 2021! My silent prayer uttered weeks before, "Lord! I really need time to spend with You', resulted in a ten-day stay in the hospital! What do you do when stress takes over your life and your body?

For educators, there is a heightened level of stress during report card windows anyway, let alone the responsibilities of pouring into the young minds of your students. Compound this as a teacher in the throes of a pandemic. Factor in a four-year separation to a spouse of 27 years, deciding whether or not to retire because teaching in a pandemic is over-the-top stressful, and the on-going concerns for an ill parent back home and a caregiver who also needs emotional and physical support? That was me! And I felt all of it!

You probably are just like me; you just push through and keep it moving even when you have a ton on your plate! Let me tell you, pushing through while carrying all that weight is costly!

With little warning that middle of January, my legs quickly spiraled along a downward path (irritating sensations inside my legs, to numbness (in my feet too), to using a cane to drag around my right leg like a dead log. What was I going to do? How was I going to teach like this? Is this what life had become for me? As things quickly worsened the next few days, I realized I had no other choice. Knocking on my son's bedroom door, through teary eyes, asked him if he'd drive me to the hospital. Two hospital visits and a neurologist appointment (with multiple tests) determined a diagnosis of Multiple Sclerosis! The thing I feared most as a child (viewing the television commercial of the woman whose hands, mouth, legs, feet, and body were bound in chains resulting from MS) stared me straight in my face! How does something like this happen to someone who eats clean and who lives a relatively healthy lifestyle? I didn't understand! It was a long, quiet trip home from the neurologist with a gazillion questions racing through my mind. Reaching home, I dragged my leg, step-by-step to my bathroom upstairs. "A l-o-n-g tub soak is what I need", I reasoned. The rug was snatched from under me. "What's gonna to happen to me, Lord?!" Until my daughter came in to the bathroom to pray with me and anointed my head, there was no peace. I'm so grateful for a praying family!

Have you been in a position where there was absolutely nothing you could do except to trust God- a difficult task for those of us who try keeping everything together? My best treatment option was a 10-day intensive alternating Apheresis Plasma Exchange and Steroids treatment in the hospital (a process by which a machine extracts the unhealthy blood and plasma from your body and replaces it with healthy artificial plasma to purify the body). This became very much a 10-day shut-in at God's feet!

I watched God orchestrate every aspect of my hospital stay. Upon arriving to WakeMed around 2:00 PM, I saw God's plan unfolding right away. He kept my son and me protected while COVID-19 was still very rampant. As I was wheeled through the emergency area, I noticed the sad, sick faces of hundreds of patients lining the hallways. God enclosed my son and me in a room inside the children's hospital and kept us safe until a room became available around 11PM that night. God had His hand on us!

The only time there was a need to be in the hospital was for the delivery of my three children. A ten-day hospital stay was very uncommon for me, with all the uncertainties of what would happen swirling through my mind! The thought of blood in any form makes me lightheaded. The awareness that there would be a large tube inserted into my neck for the exchange of healthy plasma with the old, infected blood and antibodies was a lot to fathom! My forehead beaded with sweat, as did my hands. I could have literally shaken off my hospital bed. My nerves had the best of me!

The final Apheresis Exchange treatment was scheduled for late at night in my hospital room with only one attendant, not the standard procedure. Even in this scary moment, I knew God was right there with me! This afforded me the opportunity to have a very engaging conversation with the attendant, learning about his family and life as a nephrologist. My desire always is to leave a deposit in others' lives if our paths cross, even being terrified! I thought this was an evil thing happening to me, but it wasn't. This was necessary!

This intense, unsettling time in my life became the absolute best thing that could have ever happened to me! This "shut-in" with God gave clarity to my life that I'd never had before. In my ear all day every day, I poured God's Word, motivational sermons (Bishop TD Jakes, Pastor Sarah Jakes, and Bishop Myles Monroe), and my audiobook, "The Success Principles by Jack Canfield into my ears. I craved answers from God, not just in this situation, but in every area of my life. I couldn't afford distractions. Questions I'd had for years (can my marriage be salvaged, is it time to retire, what does God want from my life) God answered right there in the hospital with precise downloaded instructions from the Lord and my Spiritual leaders. I was undergoing a metamorphosis!

How does MS happen, you might be wondering? It is primarily a hereditary autoimmune disease impacting over one million people in the US according to the National Multiple Sclerosis Society. A 2020 study published by the European Journal of Neurology, revealed that stressful adult life events (loss of a loved one, divorce, personal trauma- including childhood trauma), increased the risk factors for MS. Women are three times at greater risk than men. In my family there were no hereditary links to MS, however stress and environmental impacts were huge risk factors in my life.

I was forced to have an honest conversation with myself. How would I handle stress differently in the future so that my health isn't impacted? What's next for my life? Divorce was still very much on the table, coupled with the additional worry that (in a profession that's already very much underpaid) my livelihood could be threatened as the primary bread winner according to North Carolina Statutes where divorce is concerned. How could I handle this pressure and my dad's growing health concerns? I needed to be available if things became too progressive with Dad. Mom's growing weariness was also a looming concern for me.

Unfortunately, our patriarch took his last breath in February of 2022. My body was shouting at me, "You cannot handle stress the same way!" So, I listened. I listened to all the physicians' suggestions: medications and supplementation. I decided to become an advocate for my own health! The impact on my body resulted from environmental toxins, compounded by stress! Everything labeled caustic with warnings got dumped (cleaners, sprays, skin and hair creams, everything unhealthy). I went through a complete overhaul!

I tried to accommodate my immobile right leg in considering the purchase of a knee scooter to use when I returned to work. It dawned on me that I was absolutely "Letting life happen" to me instead of "Taking charge of it!" I became proactive! Breathwork, gratitude journaling, and meditation were additions to my daily morning devotional routine. When my body started responding to a more plant-based diet, I listened. I listened when I didn't want to exercise, but my body screamed otherwise. You do whatever is needed to take back your life because...it's your life!

Today, I am happy and healthy. My encounter with God in the hospital seeded a desire to teach families effective stress management systems; providing them resources and support because of the heightened anxiety during and post pandemic.

Life isn't stress-free, however, I'm very strategic! It was good that I was afflicted (Psalm 119:71 KJV). Life's adversities can catapult you into your Life's purpose. I'm forever changed because of it!

About the Author

Chapri Johnson has had a love for writing for as long as she could hold a pencil. She is the author of *If You Only Knew* and *More to Me Than You See*, which are soon-to-be published pieces. She inherited a love for writing from her mother, Flora Johnson, who is also an avid writer. Chapri's work is inspiring and uplifting, gifting her readers a plethora of resources to add to their toolboxes! She is one of the contributing authors in the book collaboration, *Women With Unshakeable Faith*.

Chapri resides in North Carolina with her three wonderful and supportive young adults: Viana, Ka'la, and James. Known to her colleagues as the "Child Whisperer," she is a retired elementary school teacher of thirty-two years and the founder of Proactive Positive Parenting & Partners, providing strategies and support for young families.

Connect with Chapri

- ProactivePositiveParenting@gmail.com
- Website: Chapri Johnson (canva.com)

THE FIRST RING

KRYSTAL ROSSER

What happens when God calls you and you do not answer? Are you alone in the world? Will anything bad happen for not accepting His calling? I thought God was an option! Though we attempt to find our way on our own, we always fall short and end up suffering huge consequences.

In the Bible, the Book of Jonah is a story about how Jonah refused to complete God's mission in Nineveh. Instead, he rushed away, trying to escape by getting on another ship headed the other way (Jonah 1:1-17 KJV). But God has a way of getting you where you need to be whether you accept it or not. As my grandmother used to tell me, "No matter where you are in life, God is around."

The first two times God called me, I was not a believer, and I didn't answer. I wasn't ready. I didn't want to go to church all the time. It was boring! I wanted to find God my way, but what exactly did that way look like?

I was getting my life in order, by my standards, of course. I found stable employment at a fast-food restaurant as a shift manager, I was fulfilling my educational goals as a full-time graphic design student at a local community college, and I had purchased my first car. Living at home with my grandparents, I was able to save enough money to move out on my own. I was satisfied with the quality of life I was creating for my future. Nothing indicated that my life was on the verge of unraveling.

A few months after I bought my car in 2010, I got pregnant and was diagnosed with a curable sexually transmitted infection. I was furious! I had trusted him. We had used protection. Confusion set in because my doctors had told me a month prior that I was unable to have children on my own, and that if I ever wanted to conceive, I would need medical assistance. When I was ten years old, I cried and prayed, asking God to give me a baby when I was twenty-five years old. I wanted someone that I knew would love me. I held a cassette tape called, "That's just my baby daddy." My wish came true, but if I would have taken heed to the message in the song, I might have found God faster.

After finding out about the pregnancy, I was afraid to tell my grandparents. I didn't know what they would think of me. I wasn't with the baby's father, and I contemplated terminating the pregnancy, but it wasn't an option. I knew he was a blessing from God. I vowed that I wouldn't get between my child and his father no matter what I would have to endure. But to the detriment of my life?

In the same month, I found out my grandma was dying, and I couldn't imagine losing her at the time. Emotions were all over the place, and I didn't know how to manage them or even how to feel at that point. She died when I was six months pregnant. I was alone and scared, trying to wrap my head around how my life was going to be, but I knew I couldn't lose it. After all, I was carrying another life. I didn't want to jeopardize my child's health.

My life would never be the same. I felt like a child about to have a child, and the one person I depended on had died. I was terrified. I didn't understand why God took my grandmother away from me, and I questioned God's reasons for allowing my life to be turned upside down.

The woman that had been with me since I was born was gone! What do I do? Who do I turn to? And to make matters worse, the baby's father refused to have contact with me during my pregnancy. He refused the paternity of my child. I was appalled that he would think so low of me that he would question if he was the father. My emotional and mental state collapsed right in front of my eyes.

No matter how hard life was getting, I had to keep my head up high. This was not the time to have a breakdown. I knew if I made the best choices regarding my life, things would be okay for the most part. I gave birth to my baby boy Isaiah, and his father agreed to co-parent. I wanted nothing more than for my son to have a bond with his father because I know how important both parents are to a child.

Life doesn't always go as planned, and after my son was born, things would never be the same. I initially thought co-parenting would be easy because we were both adults and we didn't have any issues going on between us. But while my back was turned, he spread malicious rumors about me. Though we didn't have any problems, he created them by lying about our relationship. I stayed in the situation because I wanted my son to grow up with his father.

I lost grip on reality, and my world spiraled out of control. I didn't have enough money to support my son, and I felt inadequate as a mother. Stressed out for not having help with my child, I fell into depression. Life had just gotten too hard with no happiness in sight. I felt confused and overwhelmed. I was lonely. I needed help. I cried for better days and felt unloved. I knew God wouldn't put me through something that would destroy my very being, but I was at my breaking point! I'd done all I could to keep my head above water. The moment I was on my knees crying out for God, he was at my door telling me to let him in! He was finished with all my antics. It was time. "Behold, I stand at the door, and knock: if any man hear my voice, and open the door, I will come in to him, and will sup with him, and he with me" (Revelation 3:20 KJV).

Before I could call out to God, I was bombarded by a heavy presence. He wasn't going to take the chance that I might ignore Him again. He banged profusely at my door for me to let Him into my heart. I didn't have a choice at this point. It was now or never. I accepted God into my life. I said, "God, I've tried everything I could possibly think of, and none of my ideas are working." I threw my hands up and shouted, "God, take the wheel! I'm done."

"Trust in the Lord with all thine heart; and lean not unto thine own understanding. In all thy ways acknowledge him, and he shall direct thy paths" (Proverbs 3:5-6 KJV). Accepting God into your life means that you will lead, live, and love in the way He has planned. For me, that meant overcoming the obstacles placed in my path to destroy my destiny, loving unconditionally, and having confidence in myself and mental clarity. When I opened my heart up to God, it felt like a huge weight had been lifted off my back. All the shame and guilt I had felt for the decisions I'd made over the years that resulted in emotional and mental anguish were gone. For the first time, I understood the situation I was in and the part I had played. I was no longer confused. God showed me ways to relieve my depression by coming out of the past. God led me to open A Clean Experience, LLC, a commercial and residential cleaning company, which alleviated my worries about providing for my child and maintaining my finances. Becoming a business owner also gave me a newfound sense of freedom that I'd never had, and I owed it to God.

Do you know what it really means to depend on God? Have faith in the Most High. The mustard seed will change your life. Learning to trust in God for every move you make means you're not taking on the world on your own. Storms come and go, but faith in God lasts forever.

DR. PAULETTE HARPER

About the Author

First-time author Krystal Rosser is a contributing author of *Women with Unshakable Faith*, which will release in April 2023. Born and raised in Toledo, Ohio, Krystal has learned to master the art of self-love. As an overcomer of childhood trauma, she understands the importance of being confident and showing up as your authentic self. She is the owner and operator of A Clean Experience, LLC, a commercial and residential cleaning company, and a single mother to an amazing little boy named Isaiah, who is her motivation for striving to better their lives. Krystal was recently featured in the *Toledo Area Parent*, a local publication for "moms who do it from home."

Connect with Krystal

- Facebook: https://www.facebook.com/krystal.r.rosser
- Website: https://krystalrosserhow.my.canva.site/

From Deliverance to Relentless

Michelle Woodson-Alexander

Have you ever been stung by a harsh, hurtful, or unbelievable statement? When that happened to me, the moment changed my life forever.

In 1982, in a bedroom, I watched sweat roll profusely down the face of an addict. I never wanted to be one. But I watched the transformation happen in a matter of seconds, and I wanted to know why, what, when, who, and how did this all begin. I remember him saying, "Don't ever try this."

Curiosity killed the cat. I begged him to let me try it. He said, "No, I don't want to be blamed for this."

"I want to try it. I won't ever blame you. I'm grown, and I'm responsible for my own actions. Let me try." I took the rock, and then I took my first hit on a glass pipe.

While exhaling, the adrenaline rushed to my head, altering my mind, body, and soul. It only lasted five to ten minutes. Then I wanted another hit. The second time, I didn't get the same head rush, and I was disappointed. I was already addicted. I could not stop, and before I knew it, eight years of chasing something I could never reach had passed. Eight long, dreadful years. There were times I wanted to stop. I prayed and cried as I went downhill.

Satan urges you to pursue things you will never catch. It was a tug-of-war, a game. I had to make a life-changing decision. Satan knew that God had his hands on me. "Watch and pray, that ye enter not into temptation: the spirit indeed is willing, but the flesh is weak" (Matthew 26:41 KJV).

Then I received a call that stung me to the core. "I will turn you in to CPS. Both of you need to stop using drugs." No intervention or conversation, no talk of rehab or getting help. "The children need you to be clean parents." At that moment, everything flashed before my eyes.

While doing drugs, my husband and I spent lots of money and lost the house we were renting. He lost his job, and I resigned from my government job. The five of us—me, my husband, and our three kids—moved into my mother's home, crammed into one bedroom. I was so ashamed to have to move back in with her, but my mother loved us enough to share her home. I am grateful for her unconditional love.

Receiving a harsh phone call from someone dear awakened me. Although my children were well taken care of by my mother, grandmother, and sisters the entire time I used drugs, one of us had to get clean and step up to raise and provide for our three beautiful black babies. I am grateful for the wonderful support system my children were embraced by during my addiction, but that phone call was my turning point. I reevaluated my life. I felt embarrassed, ashamed, and less of a mother for being a drug addict. My eight years on drugs, I labeled "The Dark Ages."

The devil had my mind so wrapped up. I told family and friends that I loved doing crack and would never quit. Sound's crazy, right? I was a size three and looked like skin and bones, but I had an aha moment.

On May 1, 1990, my husband and I decided to get clean without rehab by going cold turkey. I got so angry at myself for wasting eight years. However, I knew God was always there with me. He knew my heart and my love for Him. My life had to begin again, and I was so proud of myself. June 2, 1990, was a day I will never forget. That day, God took the taste of drugs out of my mouth. Unfortunately, it wasn't the same for my husband.

One day, I approached our bedroom. I noticed the door was closed and locked. In my gut, I knew something was wrong. I knocked. He answered with sweat flowing profusely down his face. As it did, I thought back to watching him take that hit on the glass pipe eight years before. I gagged as if I was going to throw up, and I asked him to come out of the room to the patio outside to talk.

I decided that he had to leave, and he did. I never looked back. We divorced, and I had to begin again, starting with figuring out how I could provide for my babies as well as succeed in life. I had my "come-back-to-Jesus moment" as I closed "The Dark Ages."

I challenged myself to go to cosmetology school. Even though I wondered if the drugs had altered my learning skills, I enrolled in the ten-month cosmetology school that was within walking distance from my mother's home. I shared the news with my family.

My uncle's response did not affirm my success, but his doubts challenged me to do my best. I worked hard, graduated, and passed my state board to get my cosmetology license. I did it! Not just for me but for my babies.

At my graduation, I was one of the speakers, and I shared at the ceremony what my biggest challenge was: to complete cosmetology school after being on drugs for eight years and prove to myself and others I could do it. "I can do all things through Christ which strengtheneth me" (Philippians 4:13 KJV). It was so hard to watch my uncle cry, the same man who previously doubted my success. He shared tears of joy, affirming his pride in my accomplishment on graduation day. I went on to be a single mother providing for my three children, thankful for the ten months I'd spent building my confidence to be the best I could be.

Though I never thought anyone would want me and my three children, one day, I met a man in church who changed my life forever. Because he loved me and my children unconditionally, we married after only three months. We were all blessed by God's grace and mercy. I had always hoped to be married again, and my dream came true. I just had to put my faith and trust in God. "Now faith is the substance of things hoped for, the evidence of things not seen" (Hebrews 11:1 KJV).

In church, I sang a song entitled "Press Toward the Mark," written by Norman Hutchins. That song helped me get through my recovery from crack cocaine. The words reminded me that I had to do my part in my deliverance, and God would provide forgiveness if I asked. And I love the Bible scripture that reminds me that if I reach for the stars, I can win all of life's challenges. "Brethren, I count not myself to have apprehended: but this one thing I do, forgetting those things which are behind, and reaching forth unto those things which are before, I press toward the mark for the prize of the high calling of God in Christ Jesus" (Philippians 3:13-14 KJV).

Have you ever been addicted to food, gambling, alcohol, drugs, sex, or porn? If you're reading this chapter and you or someone you may know is an addict, please tell someone what's going on and get help. Here are some resources you might want to try: Overeaters Anonymous (OA), Gamblers Anonymous (GA), Alcoholics Anonymous (AA), Narcotics Anonymous (NA), and Porn Addicts Anonymous (PAA), to name a few.

As for me, God allowed my life to prosper by becoming a business owner with my own salon as well as fulfilling my passion for photography.

About the Author

Michelle Woodson-Alexander was born in Vallejo, California. She is a mother of three and grandmother of six.

Her numerous talents include being a licensed cosmetologist and first-time co-author in the book collaboration *Woman with Unshakable Faith*, which will be released in April 2023.

She is an actress, makeup artist, singer, and photographer. Her greatest passion is her love for God, praise, and worship, the study of the Bible, and sharing her gifts and talents with others.

Michelle's musical history spans genres and audiences across America, even as far as Israel.

She has sung with notable gospel artists such as Eugene Cole and Persuaded, Gwen Pope & Friends, a duet with Edwin Hawkins and members of the NorCal chapter of the Gospel Music Workshop of America.

Connect with Michelle

- nnaychelle@yahoo.com
- FB: Michelle Woodson-Alexander
- IG: Michelle Woodson-Alexander
- YouTube: Michelle Woodson-Alexander
- Twitter: Michelle Woodson-Alexander
- Clubhouse: Michelle WoodsonAlexander
- Snapchat: Michelle Woodson-Alexander
- https://www.michellewoodsonalexandermwa.com/

The Day My Daddy Left

Christina Aguilar

What happens when you need a relationship with your father, but he isn't there?

The last time I saw my dad, he was in a casket the day we buried him. Dad wasn't around much when I was growing up. He was in and out of my life most of the time. He would send me gifts and write me letters sometimes, but it just wasn't the same. I felt alone missing him, rejected or abandoned at times, not loved. I would see other kids with their dads, but mine wasn't there. Mine was always missing.

He wasn't there all the time because he was addicted to heroin. He battled this for a long time. He lived in Los Angeles in a men's home through a church program. As a kid, I didn't understand what was happening or why he couldn't be with me. It was hard growing up without him. I always felt like something in my heart was missing: the love and presence of my dad.

When I was sixteen years old, on August 9, 2000, I got the worst news. My dad had passed away from a heroin overdose. I was eight months pregnant with my first child. My aunt came to my house to tell me. I was in shock. I felt numb. The day of his funeral was the hardest day of my life. As I walked in, I saw him lying in the casket, and I touched his cold, hard body. I sobbed because that would be the last time I would ever see him. I was so sad and hurt. I remember thinking, how will I ever get past this?

At the time of his death, not only was I pregnant with my first child, but I was also in an abusive relationship and battling depression. After my baby's birth, I resorted to using drugs and alcohol. The lifestyle I lived opened the door to me being raped, and eventually, I tried to commit suicide. But God had other ideas for my life. "He heals the brokenhearted and binds up their wounds" (Psalm 147:3 KJV).

In 2013, my aunt invited me to church with her. I said yes. But I wasn't convinced at the time that "church" was for me. When I walked through the church doors, everyone was nice to me. But I kept to myself and protected my feelings. They showed me love, but at that time, I didn't receive it. As I heard the pastor preaching his sermon, I knew God was trying to get my attention. I needed God's intervention in my life, but I wasn't sure I wanted it at that time. I was sick and tired of living in misery and wanted a different lifestyle, not only for me but for my two boys. I was so depressed that my aunt told me, "God said if you don't stop using drugs, you will die like your dad!" I didn't want my children to go through what I did when I lost my dad.

"For God so loved the world that He gave His only begotten Son, that whoever believes in Him should not perish but have everlasting life" (John 3:16 KJV). I had one foot in church and the other foot in the world. Once, I even went to church high. I don't know if anyone knew, but God knew it. I felt God telling me that not only did I have to change my heart for him, but I also had to change it for my kids. Because my kids needed me. So, I fully surrendered to God. I gave him my all. I gave him my hurt and pain. I was set free from meth, weed, alcohol, cocaine, and all my demons. He set me free from depression and low self-esteem. I started going to a twelve-step program that taught me what I needed to do, and it helped me a lot. "And He said to her, 'Daughter, your faith has made you well. Go in peace, and be healed of your affiliation'" (Mark 5:34 KJV).

God brought women into my life to encourage me, pray, and love on me. I started reading my Bible and applying it to my life. My pastor would say, "Without any challenge, there is no change," and, "Giving up is not an option." I believe that allowed me to stay focused on my new life and not turn back to my old life. Times haven't been easy, but with guidance from God and the ladies from church, I know I can make it through this life. True faith helps.

My unwavering faith would get me through everything I might face. I would pray and ask God to give me strength. I knew He loved me, and His love was real. I am His princess and His daughter, so even though my dad isn't here, my Father is always with me. He healed my broken heart and took away all the pain I felt. When I go through painful days, I look to God to get me through. I don't look to anything else but Him. "Trust in the Lord with all your heart, and lean not on your own understanding" (Proverbs 3:5 KJV).

As I look back at my life, I know it was God who really supported me. He was always there through the good times and the bad. He is my Heavenly Father, who loves me and changed my life so much. I now have a daughter, and I am a grandma. God is so good. Once you make up your mind to give it all to Him, He can do miracles in your life. He can lift you up and turn you around, put your feet on flat ground, and make you safe.

Perhaps you can relate to some parts of this. If your dad is still here but you have no contact with him, if you want a relationship, reach out. Remember, one day he may not be here, and you may go through hurt and pain because you didn't talk to or forgive one another. "And be kind to one another, tenderhearted, forgiving one another, even as God in Christ forgave you" (Ephesians 4:32 KJV).

Unforgiveness causes more pain in your life than anything else. If you are going through something like this, I am here to tell you that you are not alone. Jesus loves you so much. You can trust Him with all your heart. You can give Him all your hurt and pain. Surrender everything to Him. He wants to heal all the broken pieces. Walk by faith, not by sight or fear. I know it's hard, but with God, you can do it.

You can reach out to your nearest churches. Maybe a family member can assist you in finding a program to guide you. There are also places you can call for grieving. Talk to your doctor or your pastor. Seek help. Because there is always support. Remember, God is always there to answer prayers as well.

About the Author

Christina Aguilar is a thirty-nine-year-old mother, wife, and entrepreneur. In 2017, Christina became a first-time author featured in *Breaking Through Barriers Volume 2* and *Broken into Brilliance* volumes 1 and 2. After many trials in April of 2021, she went through a chaplain development and training program in Brentwood, California. It was then that she got her license. Through her testimonies, books, and future speaking engagements, Christina hopes to motivate others to listen to and trust the love of God. She released her newest book in December 2022, *When Queens Rise*, and it was Amazon's #1 bestseller. Christina ventured into a new business in January 2023. The name of her new business is Unique and Beautiful Boutique. She sells jewelry online. Christina feels very thankful and gives God all the glory for the wonderful changes in her life. She will be releasing her latest anthology called *Women with Unshakable Faith*, which will be released in April 2023.

Connect with Christina

DR. PAULETTE HARPER

- Email: christinaa2120@outlook.com

- Facebook: Christina Aguilar

- Website: http://Christinaaguilar.my.Canva.site

A Motherless Child

Choyce Simmons

—⁓⁓—

"A mother's love never waivers, fails, or ends, even when she is no longer with us. Her love liberates and shapes you. I am loving, compassionate, understanding, and resilient because of you, Mom. Thank you!"

As a child, was there ever something you knew you should not have done, but you did it anyway? You probably hoped you wouldn't get caught or prayed you wouldn't receive the punishment you knew you deserved. The fear of getting caught and the thought of being punished impacted how you operated moving forward. I remember hoping, "Please let my mother forget." But she never did.

Some may try to pray their way out of trouble. "Lord, if you just get me out of this situation, I promise this will be the last time." With God being the God He is, He extends His mercy, gives us grace, and saves us time and again, even when we don't deserve it. This is what makes Him such a good Father. He loves us with no limits, waits patiently for us to get our acts together, and gives us what we need, and not always what we deserve.

The loss of a parent has a profound impact on the survivors left behind. Just like when you do something you shouldn't have, when grieving a loss, you hope the pain just goes away. You may ignore the signs of grieving or grieve in an unhealthy manner, which may lead to doing things you know you shouldn't do. Studies show, "women have more profound grief responses and more difficulties adjusting to the loss of a parent than men. Most women who grieve the loss of a mother, experience challenges with self-esteem and personal growth, binge drinking, and have a high level of anxiety about becoming a mother themselves" (Center for Health and Healing, 2021).

After the loss of my mother, life hit me hard. I became my younger brother's guardian. Raising a child and being a sister were different. I tried to be the best sister I could, filling any voids my brother may have had, and protecting him from feeling any more pain than he needed to. Honestly, I had no clue what I was doing or if what I was doing was even right. I wrestled with many questions. Why had my mother been taken away from us? She was only forty-three. Where do we go from here? What was going to happen to us? How are the bills going to be paid? When is this pain going to go away? Who will comfort me as I grieve and comfort everyone else through their grief? I did not have any of the answers, and I allowed my fears to consume me, which led to more questions, insecurities, and doubts. I often had to repent my sins and ask God for forgiveness, for my thoughts and feelings did not always align with my faith and beliefs.

I knew what a good Father I served. I wanted to believe all things worked together for our good, but there were plenty of times my fear outweighed my faith. I no longer had my mother, my best friend, the one who always encouraged and motivated me when I doubted myself or wanted to give up. The scriptures did not always encourage me. "Yea, though I walk through the valley of the shadow of death, I will fear no evil" (Psalm 23:4 KJV). As powerful as that scripture is, there have been countless times I've been walking through the valley, and not only did I fear death, I feared life, the unknown, disappointment, rejection, acceptance, and so much more. Everyone and everything around me was crumbling. I wanted my life to go back to how it used to be. I wanted things to be normal, but a normal life no longer existed. I became a guardian within two months of losing my mother and a mother to my son two years later. When I gave birth to my son, my anxiety about being a mother kicked into high gear.

I was scared out of my mind to take care of two children alone when I wasn't even sure I was doing a good job taking care of myself. I felt lost, hopeless, and my faith wavered. The one person I wanted the most was no longer there. I could no longer call my mother during my time of need to get parenting advice or ask questions when I couldn't figure out how to raise these young boys. My mother used to say to me, "I pray I'm alive when you have kids of your own. I want to live long enough to see how you raise them." She did not get that opportunity, and I often wonder what she would say if she was still here.

My first question would be, "How am I doing, Mom?" The reality is, I will never know the answer, and that is a hard pill to swallow.

There are times I wonder if I am successfully fulfilling my nurturing role as a mother. Although now a motherless child, I find myself having the same parenting style as my mother, which sometimes has been a little tough to receive. So much went wrong in my life after losing my mother, and because of the grief I carried, I was on guard all the time, short-tempered, and impatient with others, even those in my home. I silently pondered what else would go wrong. What else will be taken away from us? Will I fail these boys? I wanted to be the best mother and sister-mom I could be. But I constantly questioned everything, wondering if I was parenting right, and even why it didn't seem like they loved me as I loved them. That thought cut the deepest. I knew they needed me, but I didn't think they knew how much I needed them. They were my reason for living, the motivation I needed to keep pushing through the pain.

Losing my mom left a huge void. There was a hole in my heart I thought would never be filled. My faith was weakened, and pride consumed me. I faced many circumstances I could not handle on my own, and sometimes I was afraid to call on anyone for help because I didn't want them to know how much I was struggling. For a long time, I couldn't even admit to myself or anyone that I struggled with depression. The thought of people knowing I was weak and could not control my thoughts or emotions drove me even further into isolation. Grief changes a person. It changes your energy, personality, appetite, sleep, concentration, and so much more. The enemy played with my mind. He thought he had me where he wanted me: fearful, worried, and alone. This interfered with my relationships, especially with my brother and son. I don't think they realized I had no clue what I was doing raising them. I was doing my best with what knowledge I had and learning along the way.

One day, I heard a loud voice within me say, "You are doing just fine, My child, you got this. And I am here with you every step of the way." Our Father sees and knows it all. It was when I felt weak and needed more than what others could give me that I chose to lean on and trust in Him. My grieving process was intense and personal. At times, I needed to be alone to examine myself. Being alone with God gave me the time to reflect and find peace. In my alone time, my faith grew stronger, and I decided to become one-hundred-percent dependent on God, for he would supply all my needs. His Word in Philippians 4:13 (NKJV) says, "I can do all things through Christ who strengthens me," not, "I can do all things by myself." This verse is a reminder, an encouragement, that, though life may be tough, God is with you always. I had to take many faith walks on my grief journey as a motherless child. For each step I took, one step at a time, I vowed to trust, believe, and depend on God. His strength, wisdom, courage, and peace were sufficient enough for me as a woman and mother.

"Do not remember the former things, nor consider the things of old. Behold, I will do a new thing" (Isaiah 43:18-19 NKJV). When you have lost hope, and your faith is gone, be reminded of the goodness of the Lord. Be encouraged to know how far He has brought you, and He will never leave you. God is a father to the fatherless, and a mother to the motherless. His love never fails, and His words are a beacon of light, guiding you through every part of life. Rely on Him. Trust in Him. He is a healer and provider, whatever you need, when you need Him. Believe, God is always the answer!

About the Author

Choyce Simmons is first a child of God. She's a mother to her son, an entrepreneur, and an author. Simmons is a contributing author in her first anthology, *When Queens Rise*, a #1 Amazon bestseller released December 2022, and a co-author of the latest anthology, *Women with Unshakeable Faith*, releasing April 2023.

Simmons has earned a double master's degree: one in human service counseling with a concentration in grief counseling, and the other in education with a concentration in educational therapy. Simmons also holds a certification as a grief support specialist and founded Beautiful Minds, LLC, an educational therapy, advocacy, and consulting company in 2019.

Simmons believes with true faith we can walk confidently in life knowing that God is able to carry us, sustain us, empower us, heal us, and strengthen us, no matter what.

Connect with Choyce

- Simmonschoyce@gmail.com

- www.facebook.com/ChoyceSimmons

- Website: www.iamchoycessimmons.com

BOOK REVIEWS

Did you enjoy *Women with Unshakeable Faith?* Please consider writing a book review on Amazon and Barnes & Noble.

Book reviews are important to authors and it only takes a few minutes to write one.

A review doesn't have to be long. A few short sentences or a few words to describe the book works just fine.

Book Recommendations

Since you've enjoyed reading *Women with Unshakeable Faith* will you help me promote it?

Here's how you can help.

- Kindly recommend it to books clubs and other readers.
- Ask your library to carry a copy.
- Order another copy to give away instead of passing *Women

with Unshakeable Faith around.

- Share it on social media as a book recommendation.
- Invite us to discuss the book either by Clubhouse, Facebook Live or a visit to your city.

Visionary Author Dr. Paulette Harper
www.pauletteharper.com

Thank you so much!!

WRITE A BOOK WITH ME

Do you have a story you want to share?

Would you like to be in our next anthology?

WHAT'S IN IT FOR YOU?

- Instant credibility for writing a best-selling book
- Your personal worth will increase
- Speaking opportunities will open for you
- Your personal finance will increase
- Your personal brand will be connected with other like-minded people
- Notoriety – Your circle of influence will increase and be empowered

JOIN ME!

I want to personally invite you to partner with me and join the waitlist for the next anthology offered by Visionary Author Dr. Paulette Harper

Visit https://pauletteharper.com/opportunities/ to get on the waitlist for the next book collaboration.

Author Coaching Services

Offered by Dr. Paulette Harper

Join us at One Story University Online School.

Unlock The Writer In You 90 Day Program

One Story University is an online school that provides aspiring authors with a step-by-step process on how to write and publish their self-help, how to, and personal story books in 90 days.

Visit Unlock the Writer to get access to the course.

A group coaching program for coaches, speakers, thought leaders, and entrepreneurs who are ready to write, self- publish and launch a best- selling book in 90 days.

5 Module Outline

Module 1 **The Story Framework**-The purpose behind your book, getting clarity on your story and creating the outline is the foundation every writer needs in order to produce a great book.

The best writers are those who can frame the outline of their content, ensuring each chapter flows consistently and concisely for the reader.

Module 2- **Crafting Your Story-** Writers must know their ideal audience so they craft content that compels, sells, and propels their readers. Creating a premise and promise statement assures you will achieve all three.

Module 3- **Constructing Your Book-** Putting your book all together requires knowing what goes in the front and back of your book, as well as, hiring the right literary team to help put your book together.

Module 4- **The Publishing Lab-** Now you're ready to learn the steps to finally publishing your book and securing your intellectual property.

Module 5 – **Promoting Your Book-** Before you can promote yourself and your book, you must establish a customized and focused marketing plan. Bringing a new book to the market will require a strategy, a vision and proper planning in order to generate book sales.

Other Books by Dr Paulette Harper

Do your need a self-publishing coach?
Visit https://pauletteharper.com/services/

Solo Books

Fiction Inspirational
Secret Places Revealed (Award winner)
Living Separate Lives

Children
Princess Neveah: Lessons of Self Discovery

Nonfiction
That Was Then, This Is Now: This Broken Vessel Restored
Completely Whole
Faith For Every Mountain

Coloring Book
The Scriptures in Color

Anthologies (Nonfiction)

WOMEN WITH UNSHAKABLE FAITH

The Breaking Point
When Queens Rise
For Such a Time as This
I Survived the Storm
Resilience in Hard Times
Women Who Soar
Arise From the Ashes

www.ingramcontent.com/pod-product-compliance
Lightning Source LLC
Chambersburg PA
CBHW070923160426
43193CB00011B/1560